CONSEQUENCES
OF FAILURE

BOOKS BY WILLIAM R. CORSON

Consequences of Failure
Promise or Peril: *The Black College Student in America*
The Betrayal

CONSEQUENCES
OF FAILURE

William R. Corson

W · W · NORTON & COMPANY · INC · NEW YORK

Library of Congress Cataloging in Publication Data
Corson, William R
  Consequences of failure.
     1. United States—Politics and government—1945–
2. Vietnamese Conflict, 1961–   —United States.
3. United States—Military policy. I. Title.
E839.5.C67   959.704′33′73   78–139377
ISBN 0–393–05492–6

Published simultaneously in Canada
by George J. McLeod Limited, Toronto
Printed in the United States of America
1 2 3 4 5 6 7 8 9 0

*To the memory of "Big" George A. Carroll, 1916–70,
who inspired trust and admiration as a friend and was
a professional in the finest sense of the word.*

Contents

Preface 9

1 The Phenomenon of Failure 15

2 The End in Vietnam 19

3 Military Failure: Three Case Studies 28

4 Military Failure: Ireland, 1916–22 52

5 The Military Establishment 74

6 The Cautious Government 106

7 The People 123

8 The Economy 139

9 To Overcome Failure 150

Appendix 175
Index 207

Preface

AMERICANS are beginning to look at themselves and their reaction to the Vietnam War's outcome. The present study is intended as a trial essay in this direction.

I start with what this book is not—neither a history of the Vietnam War nor a description of how the war was actually fought; both have been done well by a number of scholars and authors. Nor have I written an apologia or indictment, neither a celebration of "peace with honor" nor a lament about it.

What I have tried, rather, is to grasp—however awkwardly —the pattern and inner meaning of the phenomenon of military failure and its present and future effects on the United States, its institutions, and its people.

A personal word may not be out place. You write a book not for abstract esoteric reasons but mainly because you can't help it. This book grew out of a charge given to me in 1969 by "Big" George Carroll, to whom it is respectfully dedicated. At the time —shortly before President Nixon's inauguration—he was leaving Washington to return to the field of education after a government career that included combat service in World War II and Korea as an infantry commander; the front lines of the Cold War in Iran and West Germany as the senior CIA official in charge of clandestine operations; service as Special Assistant for Counterinsurgency in the Office of International Security Affairs; and finally, from 1965 to 1969, service as Special Assistant to Vice President Humphrey on National Security Affairs. George told me: "One day the war will be over, and it is important that we don't let its aftereffects destroy our faith in our country and our ability to overcome past mistakes." This I have tried to do.

Whatever I have written, thought, or felt in the past about America's problems with war and peace has converged on the theme of the nature and meaning of our military failure in Vietnam. No American, perhaps no one alive today, can pretend to view the consequences of that failure with complete emotional detachment. The best you can do to achieve perspective is to keep a certain emotional distance from your subject. When the subject is your own nation and its institutions it is hard to keep the distance. Your hopes and fears for America manage to show through and color the analysis.

Obviously any book about America's reaction to the fact of our military failure in Vietnam at a time when it is still a matter of public debate is bound to be interpreted within the frame of concern, and the question will be asked what this book is "for" or "against." I have tried to avoid this dead end. I love my country, but it is no service to it, nor to its people, to gloss over the rough facts of the consequences of our mistakes. If there are some consequences I have not confronted, it has not been through lack of diligence or realism, but because I have tried to focus on the most important ones and their related aspects. In dealing with something so provocative and demoralizing as failure it is easy to get thrown off the track by the transient and miss the enduring and significant. Our purpose should be to try to overcome the consequences of failure, and it is to that end that this book has been directed.

During the period in which this book was written I owe acknowledgments to Eric Swenson, Vice President of W. W. Norton & Company, who went far beyond his duty as publisher in order to help lick the book into shape, and especially to Georgia Griggs, to whom fell much of the burden of preparing the book for press.

I want to thank John Cushman, my agent, for reading and and criticizing the larger portion of the book, although I am certain it still falls far short of his exacting standards, and for his encouragement at several critical junctures.

Finally, I want to say how much I owe to my wife, Judith, for her patience with my moody preoccupations during the writing of this book, but who kept me at the task and retained her belief in what must have seemed at times a monstrously demoralizing venture.

William R. Corson

Potomac, Maryland
April 1973

CONSEQUENCES
OF FAILURE

ONE

The Phenomenon of Failure

"If we take from history the discussion of why, how, and wherefore each thing was done and whether the result was what we should reasonably have expected, what is left is a clever essay but not a lesson, and while pleasing for the moment of no possible benefit for the future."

—Polybius

IN THE historical evolution of the American people there have been four major crises, each of which we either surmounted out of our own spiritual and physical resources or were rescued from by virtue of outside events: the birth of a viable government in 1789, slavery and the trauma of ending it, the moral obligation of membership in the League of Nations, and the Great Depression of 1929. And now there is a fifth, the challenge to deal with the consequences of our failure in Vietnam in the world at large, in Asia, in Vietnam, and most importantly here at home.

Victory and how to achieve it has proved to be a fascinating subject for study by a wide variety of scholars, politicians, and soldiers. The psychology of failure or, if you will, the consequences of failure to those who believed in the certainty of their victory has received relatively little attention.

Failure—the nonperformance of something required or expected—is not an uncommon experience in the life of a nation. The histories of even the most successful nations provide ample evidence of widespread dissatisfaction and failures in the face of certain successes. Failure is not confined to any single period of a nation's history, nor is there a period without it. Although failure does not always follow the disruption of the best-laid plans of soldiers and politicians, neither does success in one or several aspects of a situation necessarily preclude overall failure. Sometimes partial triumphs only sow the seeds of final failure.

The dynamic processes involved in national failure have remained obscure. It has been dealt with by historians as a symbolic abstraction in their chronicles of civilizations and by biographers in their treatment of the lives of those who have significantly influenced human events, and it has been the theme of legends, myths, folk stories, and songs.

As a national social phenomenon, failure has been studied almost exclusively in terms of the narrow perspectives of victory or defeat. The consequences of national failure, which comprise not only the fact of failure itself but the emotions associated with it, both influence and are influenced by the nation's psychological maturity and development. Thus, failure is as much a determinant of future political behavior as is success. The unpleasantness and pain that failure causes may account for its neglect as a subject of investigation, as if acknowledging it is to admit something shameful. However, the U.S. failure in Vietnam will be easier to accept and learn from if we can see it in terms of its predictable consequences on the main components of society, institutional and social.

It is too pat to blame the failure in Vietnam on a selected few, or on all of us in order to dismiss its consequences. It is only meaningful in a historical context that relates it to the fact that since 1945 we have been living in a new age, endlessly embracing our recent enemies in the dubious consolation of mutual deterrence. Vietnam caught us overconfident of our new firepower, which proved to be more materially destructive than it had been advertised but politically inadequate. "Search and destroy" as practiced by U.S. forces in Vietnam sums up this inadequacy, but not its social and psychological effects on those who had to carry it out or on those at home who could only look on in horror.

For those who believe in their country, the spectacle of

America being wantonly destructive in Vietnam, being pushed around by its allies and dishonored by its own soldiers, was a highly traumatic experience, since a devaluation of national identity is a loss affecting the very quality of life itself. A few years ago discussion of these situations seemed fanciful, if not treasonous, but the war has been a shock to most established habits of military, social, and political thinking. There has been a slow but sure change of sentiment, among ordinary men, about these things, and that is one of the consequences of failure.

The truth about how America became involved in the Vietnam conflict is beginning to come out. The Pentagon Papers are in the public domain. Numerous authors, each with varying degrees of responsibility for American involvement and the subsequent conduct of the war, are "telling it like it was" . . . or, in retrospect, at least how it appeared from their individual vantage points. From these separate accounts a grotesque chain of events has been revealed, each link providing the means to forge the next. None of these accounts, either taken singly or together, provides a complete explanation of why the war began and why it was continued for so long, nor do they explain why those responsible policy makers who ultimately came to oppose the war or who later said they had been opposed to it all along did not publicly oppose it when their opinion might have made a difference.

It is not our purpose here to address the "why" questions, or to provide a revisionist history of the Vietnam War and the successive missed opportunities to end or avoid it entirely, or to concern ourselves with what is likely to happen next in Vietnam. Obviously, it helps to know what happened and why, but such analyses will find a more receptive audience after the country has had time to recover from the shock of the war and is more willing to look at it objectively.

It *is* our purpose to judge and evaluate the consequences of America's military failure in Vietnam in terms of its observable and predictable effects upon the United States and its institutions. There can be no evasion or delay in undertaking this onerous task if future Vietnams are to be avoided and, more importantly, if America is to survive and attempt to overcome the consequences of this failure. Ours is not the judgment of history nor of the Oracle of Delphi, but rather a straightforward attempt to give all Americans an explanation of why wars like the Vietnam War are fought, why America and other nations have failed in that kind of war, and what are the foreseeable consequences to American society of such a failure. The war has ended for America, but bitterness and a sense of national betrayal remain. The necessity for thinking Americans to judge the results of our failure will not go away, because the war has revealed and caused too many problems to just ignore its consequences. A generation ago, in its frustration, the United States turned on itself, and Joe McCarthy exploited that mood to divide the nation and pit the Congress against the chief executive. It could happen again.

If we now, as a consequence of the publication of the Pentagon Papers, have a complete documentary record of the U.S. attempt at preserving the fiction of South Vietnam as a nation and of the abhorrent perversity that accompanied it, have we a similar clear vision of America's soul and America's mind? It will not suffice to limit ourselves to condemnation of the patent iniquity of our involvement in Vietnam; the process of reconstructing America demands a solid foundation of intellectual honesty, moral integrity, and mastery of self. This is not to denigrate in any way the importance of such questions as "What will America's role in Asia be now?" or "How do we help rebuild what we have helped destroy?" but rather to emphasize that we shall repeat our failure in Vietnam elsewhere unless this examination of conscience is carried out at home.

TWO

The End in Vietnam

> "After ten years' war with perpetual success, to tell us
> it is yet impossible to have a good peace is very surpris-
> ing, and seems so different from what has happened in
> the world before, that . . . it is natural to inquire into
> our present condition; how long shall we be able to go
> on at this rate; what the consequences may be upon the
> present and future ages; and whether a peace without
> impracticable point . . . be really ruinous in itself or
> equally so with the continuance of the war."
> —Jonathan Swift

EACH PRESIDENT from Truman to Johnson turned over to his suc-
cessor a more serious problem in Southeast Asia. Truman gave
Eisenhower a situation in which U.S. arms and equipment had
prolonged the French in their colonial war long after they would
have been thrown out by the Vietnamese. Eisenhower left Kennedy with a totalitarian dictator who could neither rule South
Vietnam nor conquer North Vietnam even though the United
States had given him a superabundance of military equipment.
Kennedy left Johnson a burgeoning guerrilla war that no one in
his administration knew how to either fight or avoid. And Johnson turned over to Nixon a hopeless "no win and everything to
lose" military and political situation. Thus the cumulated mismanagement and misperceptions relating to Vietnam were
dropped on President Nixon, who finally chose to end the political and military madness.

President Nixon's choice was a difficult one. It meant that he
had to concede that we could not do what we set out to do in

Vietnam by the application of all-but-unlimited military power. It forced him to risk the danger that if the fact of our military failure was improperly perceived at home and abroad it would bring about additional political and military problems. The risks were real. There was no assurance that he could maintain control over the military if his acknowledgment of its failure in Vietnam was used by others to indict individuals for their human frailties and personal responsibilities *in* that failure. The issue was further complicated because he could not reveal all the reasoning behind his decision, which might have foreclosed the few remaining options for getting out of Vietnam without incurring the additional risks of a wider war and increased tension at other danger points. He knew that to get out of Vietnam was going to be an exceedingly complex task and that if he failed in it, the consequences of that failure to the United States and its institutions would far outweigh those associated with our military failure in the war itself. And he required the cooperation of those for whom admitting that we had failed was a complete anathema.

From President Nixon's acknowledgment of the fact of military failure flowed his subsequent decision about how to actually get out of Vietnam. It was a complicated one. It is to his credit that he did not opt to get out immediately and precipitately in February 1969, when he was presented with a golden political opportunity to do so. At that time Senators Fulbright and Mansfield offered their support—and promised to help overcome partisan criticism—if Nixon would take Senator Aiken's advice to "declare a victory and get out." The Fulbright-Mansfield offer was a serious one, based on painstakingly detailed analyses made by members of the Senate Foreign Relations Committee's staff and others formerly associated with the reality of the situation. The analyses all came to the same inescapable conclusions: that there was no way the United States could turn South Vietnam into a viable independent political entity, and all that could be achieved by staying in the war would be to keep a so-called anti-Communist military government temporarily in power in South Vietnam; that the result of continued U.S. presence in Vietnam—aside, of course, from the frightful cost in American lives and money—would be the almost complete destruction of the entire Vietnamese social fabric for several generations; and that to destroy the people of South Vietnam in order to save them from a "fate worse than death" just didn't make any sense at all.

Because these conclusions did not square with anything that candidate Nixon, nominee Nixon, and President-elect Nixon had been told about the situation in Vietnam, *President* Nixon ordered Henry Kissinger to find out the truth in the matter. Kissinger's response was National Security Study Memorandum (NSSM) Number 1, in which he asked various government agencies to give him their views about the conduct of the war. By approaching the agencies separately and giving them a chance to damn others with faint praise or point an accusatory finger at their competitors, it was possible to get a reasonably accurate estimate of the actual situation in, and the prognosis for, Vietnam.* The result supported the studies done for Fulbright and Mansfield, which convinced Nixon that it was time to get out.

Once the decision was made known within the government, disagreement erupted among those with a proprietary interest in the war about how—and how fast—it should be accomplished. Old schisms surfaced. The military was divided over whether withdrawal should be based on the tactical combat situation or tied to the "progress" of the Vietnamization program, and the military's hawks did their best to persuade Nixon to reconsider his decision and seek a military victory. However, politically minded generals quickly got on board the "Vietnamization Express." Rationalization for this approach was provided by General Maxwell D. Taylor, in a March 10, 1971, *New York Times* article entitled "Let's Unite on Vietnamization": "Since our involvement in Vietnam, there have been only three strategic alternatives from which to choose—to advance, to retreat, or to stand fast—although variants may be formed from elements of

---

* See the appendix for the text of NSSM 1 and a draft summary of the responses to its questions.

all three. Unfortunately, since 1967 it has been impossible to rally public opinion behind any one of these alternatives. To advance offends the doves, to retreat offends the hawks, and to stand fast exasperates the impatient who constitute the national majority."

Taylor's call to unity on Vietnamization was seen by some military officers as a way to continue to fight the war with proxy forces in order to pursue the "victory" that had eluded them with their own forces. But that was not Nixon's purpose; he used Vietnamization as a face-saving device to cover the withdrawal of U.S. forces and to add a fourth strategic alternative: "to ignore"—that is, to disregard extraneous events over which he had no direct control and not allow them to influence his responses. It is interesting to note that the principles underlying U.S. Vietnam policy since 1969 are set forth in considerable detail in the writings of Henry Kissinger. I mention this not to imply that Kissinger rather than Nixon made the basic decisions, but to point out that the affinity between their ideas and approach is very great and that Nixon's policies are grounded in long-range theory and are not merely the result of political expediency.

Nixon adopted the "to ignore" strategy and coupled it with alternate offers and threats in the diplomatic arena and alternate lunges and lulls in the military arena. His game plan went like this:

Diplomacy (offer): In the spring of 1969, Nixon outlined his proposals for ending the war, including mutual withdrawal, a cease-fire with international supervision, and free elections in South Vietnam.*

Diplomacy (threat): On April 20, 1970, Nixon reiterated his determination to take "strong and effective measures if increased enemy action in Laos, Cambodia, or South Vietnam jeopardized the security of our remaining forces." †

Military (lunge): Cambodia was invaded at the end of April.

* Department of State Bulletin, June 2, 1969.
† Department of State Bulletin, April 20, 1970.

Military (*lull*): Although fighting continued in Cambodia, American ground troops were removed by June 30, 1970.

Diplomacy (*offer*): The American negotiating team in Paris got its new chief, David K. Bruce, who was appointed on July 1 and took over in Paris a month later. On October 26 Nixon announced a "new" peace plan. Instead of free elections, he proposed a political settlement according to the will of the South Vietnamese people, recognizing the existing relationship of forces, with the United States to abide by whatever political process was agreed to. Cease-fire and withdrawal proposals remained the same. Two new points were added: an Indochina Peace Conference, to include Laos and Cambodia, and immediate and unconditional release of all prisoners of war on both sides.*

Military (*lunge*): This proposal was unacceptable to the North Vietnamese and the National Liberation Front. To underscore the importance he attached to it, Nixon ordered the attempt to rescue American POWs held in North Vietnam's Son Tay prison camp, and the renewed bombing of the North. Beyond its immediate objective, the prisoner rescue raid was also designed to convey Nixon's intentions in two other areas. First, it defused a sensitive political issue and provided further justification for staying in the war as long as there was a single prisoner of war held in North Vietnam. Second, it served as a potent warning to the North Vietnamese that their territory was subject to invasion, a warning that was shortly conveyed more explicitly. The renewed bombing was accompanied by another threat.

Diplomacy (*threat*): In his press conference on December 10, 1970, Nixon warned the North Vietnamese that if the U.S. reconnaissance planes were fired upon, he would "not only order that they return the fire, but . . . that the missile site be destroyed and that the military complex around that site which supports it also be destroyed by bombing." He added that if U.S. ground forces remaining in South Vietnam were threatened by North Vietnamese infiltration, he would "order the bombing of military sites in North Vietnam, the passes that lead from

* Department of State Bulletin, October 26, 1970.

North Vietnam into South Vietnam, the military complexes, and the military supply lines." *

Military (preparations): The war in Laos was intensified in late 1970 and early 1971. In mid-December the Pathet Lao reported stepped-up fighting in the plain of Jarres, and North Vietnam charged that more Thai troops were being sent to the Bolovens plateau and Long Cheng. Early in January 1971 the U.S. Air Force was reported to be preparing for possible retaliatory attacks against their Thailand bases, and B-52 raids along the Laos-North Vietnam border were increased.†

Diplomacy (threat): At the Paris negotiations on February 5, Bruce said that the United States would carry out "alternative solutions to the conflict" unless serious peace negotiations were begun.‡

Military (lunge): Laos was invaded by South Vietnamese forces with heavy U.S. support on February 8.

Diplomacy (signals to China): In his State of the World message on February 25, 1971, Nixon proposed trade and "serious dialogue with the People's Republic of China"—the first time an American President had ever referred to Communist China by its proper name. This, in addition to Nixon's explicit statements, was a clear signal that there was no threat to China in the Laos invasion. However, almost immediately Chou En-lai and some of his top aides went to Hanoi—a signal that China took the Laos invasion very seriously. A final signal was sent in this exchange when Nixon lifted U.S. travel restrictions to China and hinted that there might be rewards for China if she stayed out of the Laos situation.

Military (lull): The Laos "incursion" ended in a complete rout. There was little doubt that Vietnamization was far from complete as the ARVN forces straggled out of Laos on foot, hanging from the skids of U.S. helicopters, and cowering inside the U.S. armored vehicles dispatched to rescue them. They were clearly ineffective on their own against a determined enemy. Had

---

* Department of State Bulletin, December 11, 1970.
† Chronology from U.S. and French news sources.
‡ Department of State Bulletin, February 5, 1971.

the Laos invasion been successful, the next steps would have been predictable: another military lull, another offer of settlement on the same or similar terms as those outstanding, and, if they were not accepted, heavier bombing of the North, perhaps accompanied by ARVN and/or U.S. amphibious raids in North Vietnam.*

The failure of the Laos incursion was most important. In conformity with the "to ignore" strategy, it signaled the end of South Vietnam as a determining factor, or any kind of a real influence, in the negotiations being pursued by Kissinger with the North Vietnamese. South Vietnam's military and political leaders mistakenly thought they still had some hold over the United States, but as far as Nixon and Kissinger were concerned the government of South Vietnam had been irrevocably demoted to the position of a pawn in their game of foreign-policy chess. Hence the President's decision to go to Peking.

Probably nothing has made it more difficult to understand, or even recognize, Nixon's application of the "to ignore" strategy than the zigzagging language employed by the President and other administration officials as they sought to portray a "winding down" of the American involvement in the conflict. Although Nixon reduced the American ground-combat role in South Vietnam and its consequent casualties, American helicopters and B-52s took a heavier beating during the Laos incursion than at any stage of the war except during the bombing of North Vietnam in December 1972. This, plus the fact that Cambodia flanks South Vietnam to the west, augurs ominously for a situation that could result in the necessity to increase the commitment of U.S. air power, or reintroduce U.S. ground-combat forces, to prevent the loss of Laos and Cambodia if the cease-fire agreement be-

---

* Although such raids were not carried out, confirmation that they had been actively considered by the United States was provided by Admiral Thomas H. Moorer, chairman of the Joint Chiefs of Staff, in closed-door testimony before two House Appropriations subcommittees on January 9 and 18, 1973, in the aftermath of the "carpet bombing" B-52 raids on North Vietnam in December, but before the cease-fire agreement was announced later in January. In the testimony made public, Admiral Moorer said that the Joint Chiefs had actually "recommended" a flanking movement that would have involved a land invasion of the North.

comes unstuck. And such a result also seriously threatens Thailand.

Thus Nixon's de-escalation of America's military role in South Vietnam was more apparent than real because the reduction of ground-combat forces was more than compensated by the escalation of the U.S. air-combat role and "proxy" control over the Cambodian and Laotian forces in a wider war. The Nixon administration would like us to believe that the 51,189-ton increase in bombing in the first three Nixon years over the last three Johnson years was effective against North Vietnamese and Viet Cong operations in South Vietnam,* but there is nothing to show that it impeded their operations in Laos and Cambodia. This and the fact that the "success" of South Vietnamese, Cambodian, and Laotian forces in combat against those of North Vietnam has either been illusory or marked by Italian-type advances to the rear indicated that further gradations of force were considered necessary by Nixon and Kissinger to produce a a satisfactory settlement of the war.

On a purely personal basis, I believe that Nixon's decision about why and how to end our involvement in Vietnam was the right one. One can quibble over details, or raise the "bloody shirt" of twenty thousand dead Americans, or argue that it took too long. However, as indicated by NSSM 1, it was a complicated decision made more so because of the necessity to gain control over the situation before Nixon could get the troops safely out and in so doing not create another set of conditions that would

---

* "U.S. Air War in Vietnam," Cornell University, Center for International Studies, Ithaca, N.Y., November 1971. The report, done principally by nineteen scholars with Professor Raphael Littauer as coordinator, indicates that Pentagon figures show 552,292 tons of bombs dropped from January through August 1971. Adding that amount to the 977,446 tons dropped in 1969 gives a grand total of 2,916,997 tons of bombs under President Nixon, more than the 2,865,808 tons listed by the Pentagon for 1966 through 1968 when Rolling Thunder raids were flown against North Vietnam. Since then, "protective reaction" strikes against North Vietnam, support of South Vietnamese and Cambodian troops, and the heavy bombing of Laos, especially along the Ho Chi Minh trail, have kept the bombing tonnage high during the Nixon administration. It was further estimated that the bombs dropped during the eleven-day B-52 "carpet bombing" raids in December 1972 came to slightly less than a million tons.

have forced him to re-escalate the war. He was right to proceed in a deliberate, controlled fashion. To have done otherwise would have been more imprudent and irresponsible than it was for his predecessors to ignore the economic, political, and military realities of Vietnam, which only created more problems.

The full record of the extremely tense negotiations with the North Vietnamese between October 25, 1972, and January 24, 1973, and of Nixon's decision on December 17, 1972 calling for the "carpet bombing" of North Vietnam by B-52s—as well as that of the three and a half years of secret negotiations—will probably be told only after the President has decided that revealing the details will not resurrect the issue of Vietnam. This war will provide a remarkable case study of how "little" decisions lead to big problems. It will be unfortunate if we as a nation are so eager to forget Vietnam that the war—and especially Nixon's management of the withdrawal from it—does not receive the rigorous analysis it deserves, because it would deny us of an important opportunity to understand and learn from the methods by which executive decisions are made.

THREE

Military Failure: Three Case Studies

"They conquered heaven by force of arms because heaven suffers violence, but as for me, I don't know to this moment what it is that I conquer by force of my feats and travail. If my Dulcinea del Toboso could be freed from her own travails, and my fortune were to improve and my wits be mended, it might be that I could tread a better path than the one I'm on."
—Cervantes, *Don Quixote*

EVEN THOUGH President Nixon's plan of withdrawal from Vietnam was perhaps the best that could be devised under the circumstances, any feeling that the United States has achieved a moral victory—a "happy ending" after all—is an illusion. In this chapter we will review some earlier cases of military failure that may help us understand our present condition and acknowledge the fact of our own failure in spite of any official pronouncements to the contrary.

Our intention is to point out how violating or ignoring certain principles of "limited war" strategy contributes to the failure of a great power in a conflict not directly affecting its national existence. These principles are based as much on social considerations as they are on technical ones, and they require an understanding of the moral as well as the physical limits of a nation's war-making power.

Clausewitz' complex notion of how to judge the outcome of a war is relevant in this case, as opposed to General MacArthur's dictum that there is no substitute for victory. As Clausewitz pointed out, winning means either to achieve one's political and strategic objectives by offensive action or, defensively, to thwart the enemy's intentions; losing means failure to achieve one's objectives *even though* one's forces are undefeated and still able to engage the enemy.* The American experience of the Spanish-American war and the two world wars, wherein the "enemy" countries acknowledged total defeat and surrendered their independence and sovereignty, has left the United States psychologically unprepared for a military loss in the Clausewitzian sense in any war, especially a limited one.

In victory there is joy. In defeat—even complete national defeat—there may be solace in having fought the "good fight." In the *failure* to achieve the expected military decision there is neither joy nor solace. So far in our national history—aside from a temporary setback such as the loss of the Philippines in 1942—we have been spared both the psychological shock that accompanies a military defeat and the necessity to make a comeback in the face of occupation by an outside power. The idea of military defeat is so alien to the perceptions of the American people, or, if you will, their national psyche, that it has not even commanded any serious attention as a theme for speculative historical fiction.

The phenomenon of military failure differs significantly from military defeat in form and substance; even more importantly, it is different in its effect on the socioeconomic and political fabric of the nation. Unlike defeat, failure follows a highly consistent pattern, varying only in how long it takes to run its course. The country where the war is actually fought is usually far away

---

* Henry A. Kissinger, "The Vietnam Negotiations," *Foreign Affairs*, January 1969, p. 214. "The North Vietnamese and Vietcong, fighting in their own country, needed merely to keep in being forces sufficiently strong to dominate the population after the U.S. tired of the war. We fought a military war; our opponents fought a political one. We sought physical attrition; our opponents aimed for our psychological exhaustion. In the process we lost sight of one of the cardinal maxims of guerrilla war: *the guerrilla wins if he does not lose* [italics added]. The conventional army loses if it does not win. The North Vietnamese used their armed forces the way a bullfighter uses his cape—to keep us lunging in areas of marginal political importance."

and is "foreign" in the sense of its ideological or religious orientation and/or its ethnic make-up, and the initiating cause of the
war is usually not the conventional one of conquest for territory
or natural resources.

Military failure occurs in stages, beginning with a recognition on the part of a nation's leaders that there is a limit to the
military power available for the venture or that the physical condition in the embattled country precludes the effective use of all
the available military strength. Then follows a disillusioned withdrawal of the public's moral support for the men doing the fighting and bafflement over the enemy forces' resoluteness as more
firepower is directed against marginal military targets. This produces a general weariness with the war along with the realization
by the people that it is easier to get into military adventures than
to get out, and a frantic search by the political leaders for a diplomatic gimmick to make the failure look like a victory or to
divert public attention to another issue. Paralleling this development there emerges a series of divisive domestic crises that
exacerbate relations among all groups in the society and make
the failing nation's social problems more difficult, if not impossible, to solve. Without exception, the convergence of these elements produces a marked change in the nation's view of future
foreign affairs and in its basic orientation to its domestic policies.

To fit professional fighting forces into the operations of the
body politic has long been a delicate procedure. Generally, political leaders feel it is necessary to maintain standing armies to
carry out distant imperialistic types of operations, which is one
of the characteristics of military failure, but this kind of operation has historically been beyond the scope of nonprofessional
citizen armies. According to Herbert Fisher, the decision to
change from a nonprofessional to a professional standing army
was first faced by the Roman republic two thousand years ago
when Marius (*c.* 155–86 B.C.) decided to stop using peasants for
summer campaigns, after which they returned to their farms, and
reorganized the Roman army into a standing force of professional

soldiers.* As a consequence, Rome had the military means to create and then expand the Roman Empire, which in turn prompted the arrogant belief on the part of Rome's leaders that their armies were all-powerful. This set the psychological stage for a military failure, followed by the decline and fall of the empire.

There is no simple formula to adequately account for the failure of Rome's leaders to perceive that there were limits to Roman military power. Augustus, the first of the Roman emperors, succumbed to the myopia induced by relatively easily and cheaply achieved military success, beginning with the Battle of Actium in 31 B.C., after which he was able to add Egypt to the provinces of Rome, keeping it under his own personal supervision. In 27 B.C. Augustus took charge of the frontier provinces and, in keeping with the almost automatic imperial thrust that seems to follow a successful military conquest, strove to secure natural boundaries for them. This resulted in further expansion . . . and so on. For example, when the northwestern tribes of Spain were subdued (27–24 B.C.) the entire Iberian peninsula came under Roman rule.

The lack of significant opposition to these conquests led Augustus to believe there was no limit to his power and that it was possible to occupy the territories conquered by Rome while simultaneously expanding the empire by additional conquests. This conclusion was proved false by the horrendous results of Augustus' decision to extend the empire's western frontier from the Rhine to the Elbe in A.D. 4, when he ordered his stepson, Tiberius, to invade the German tribal lands and destroy the tribes' armed bands. By A.D. 5 Tiberius had reached the Elbe and Germany had been brought into the empire—or so it was made to appear in Rome. However, in response to a major revolt in the province of Pannonia in A.D. 6, Tiberius formed an attack force from part of his occupation troops, which so weakened the occupation level that guerrilla activities erupted in the "pacified"

---

* Herbert A. L. Fisher, *A History of Europe*, Lawrence Verry, Mystic, Conn., 1971, Vol. I, p. 71.

tribal areas. Augustus wanted to send reinforcements to Tiberius, but the combination of time, distance, and a Roman professional military manpower shortage made it impossible.

Meanwhile, back at the Rhine, where Tiberius had left Publius Quintilius Varus with three legions to guard Rome's border and protect his rear, Roman "carpetbaggers" were straggling back with tales of guerrilla uprisings. Varus, apparently afflicted with the same kind of megalomania displayed by General George C. Custer in a similar situation before the battle of the Little Big Horn, decided to teach the "natives" a lesson. On his own recognizance he took the entire Rhine garrison on a march designed to entice the Germans to attack his force. In the depths of a barely penetrable forest, someplace between Osnabruck and Detmold, he got his wish. The Germans ambushed Varus and his troops, killing all but a handful of the Romans. A few survivors were allowed to return to Rome to tell the story of the battle, but Varus chose to commit suicide rather than face the consequences.

The moral of this story is not only that an inferior force with an intimate knowledge of the terrain could overcome a better-armed and better-organized military force; it also has to do with the social, psychological, and political principles revealed as a result of this defeat. Since Augustus was unwilling to publicly acknowledge that Varus had acted unwisely and that the army was overextended, Rome's leaders and people perceived Varus' *defeat* as a *failure;* they then became alarmed and lost confidence in *all* the Roman legions. This reaction was strong enough to cause Augustus to abandon his imperial expansionist policy in favor of retrenchment and to face the fact that there were limits to the effective military strength of Rome. Augustus' policy change supports our view that military failure—whether it is correctly perceived or not—produces a social, psychological, and political reaction well out of proportion to the objective facts of the failure. In this case, aside from emotional shock at the defeat of Varus, one of Rome's "great" commanders, the loss of three legions was not all that important except that it occurred during one of the periodic recruitment and manpower crises that seem to be endemic to nations with far-flung "commitments."

The lessons learned by Augustus "stayed learned" until the reign of Trajan (A.D. 98–117), who once again set Rome off on imperialistic expansionist policy, this time to the east rather than the west. Trajan's decision to move against forces Rome had never faced in battle is a manifestation of the kind of chauvinism that equates "foreign" customs, religions, or races with inferior military ability and lack of courage. Trajan, like his predecessors, achieved easy early victories in the First (A.D. 101–2) and Second (A.D. 105–6) campaigns against Dacia, located between the Carpathian mountains and the Danube, an area corresponding to modern-day Rumania and its contiguous regions.

The Dacian conquest provided Rome with rich booty, of which more than a third was given to the urban poor as a "bonus" for their support of the war.* Most of the remainder was used to finance Trajan's extensive public-works program, which reduced unemployment and the necessity for charity. Furthermore, the people of Dacia welcomed settlers from Rome and were pleased that the legions of Rome had assumed the responsibility for their defense. The frosting on Trajan's cake was the fact that the gold mines of Dacia provided him with the means to refill Rome's empty treasury and restore public confidence in the government—no mean feat when one considers that two of his predecessors were the infamous Caligula and Nero.

But Trajan's satisfaction with his imperial success in Dacia was relatively short-lived. Unlike Augustus, who overestimated Rome's military strength and became greedy, Trajan was like a man who has won the hand of the world's most beautiful woman and is now afraid his lecherous neighbors will try to steal her away from him. He changed his "good neighbor" policy toward Dacia's neighboring "independent and friendly" states to one of direct involvement in and control over their internal affairs. At first, this policy seemed wise; in A.D. 114 Trajan annexed Armenia

* Tenney Frank, *An Economic Survey of Ancient Rome,* Octagon, N.Y., 1972, Vol. 3, pp. 130–32.

almost as easily as Hitler took over Czechoslovakia in 1938. Then, in 115, he decided to invade Parthia (now a part of northeastern Iran). Parthia's leaders refused to acknowledge Roman suzerainty and warned Trajan that if he invaded their country they would destroy him and his legions.

Trajan's Parthian campaign provides a good example of the physical conditions that generally accompany the phenomenon of military failure. At the start, Trajan's legions had a 10 or 12 to 1 numerical superiority over the Parthian field forces, were much better armed and equipped, and had a horse-drawn wheeled-vehicle logistical force at their disposal. By avoiding pitched battles and using guerrillas to harass the Romans and cover their retreat, the Parthians lured Trajan and his legions deeper and deeper into the vast spaces of Parthia, with predictable results: the Romans' superiority was dissipated in guarding lines of communication, manning the garrison forts, and attempting to resupply their strung-out attack forces. Their "positional conquest"—the ground they physically occupied—lasted until A.D. 117, when a reorganized Parthian field force selected the least combat-ready, farthest-extended legion and attacked it by surprise. Then, thanks to their guides and guerrillas, who kept them informed of the positions of the heads of the legions' columns, they slipped in between the strongest of the legions in forced day and night marches. Finally, they attacked the weakest of the remaining columns. They kept this up until Trajan sounded the retreat and gave up, one by one, the Parthian territories he had sought to control.

Trajan's death on his way back to Rome spared him from facing the domestic consequences of his military failure, which are especially interesting to us because they provide the first clear illustration of the kinds of social problems military failure either produces or aggravates. While Trajan was pursuing the Parthians, the major domestic problems of Rome, such as welfare, loans to farmers, and the cost ineffectiveness of slave labor, had to be set aside. In spite of the booty acquired in Dacia, Trajan's Rome didn't have enough resources to pursue a "guns and butter" policy. Unlike the short, profitable Dacian campaigns, the war in Parthia dragged on and made increasing demands on manpower and resources that could only come from those previously allocated by Trajan to meet Rome's domestic needs. The results show how quickly—even in a highly regimented society—the social fabric of a nation can become unraveled. By A.D. 117 the heartland of Rome was on the verge of civil war, and political unrest in the provinces and nations that Rome had annexed through conquest was heightened by the evidence of the military failure in Parthia. As a general proposition, we may conclude that once a dominating national power sustains a military failure its "allies" become less tractable and are likely to strike out on their own or try to make a deal with another power.

Hadrian, who succeeded Trajan, recognized this proposition and its obvious corollary—that after the fact of a military failure attempts to continue with all of a nation's previous commitments were bound to fail because of public pressure to cut the amount of money spent for military purposes. As a consequence, Hadrian abandoned Trajan's expansionist policy, contracted the empire back to a defensible size, gave up the idea of conquering all of Britain, and substituted "technology" for manpower where feasible to defend Rome's frontiers. For example, he constructed the famed Hadrian Wall across the narrow neck of Britain between Carlisle and Wallsend, which enabled him to reduce the size of the Roman garrison in Britain by more than half. Before anyone dismisses Hadrian's notion of "Fortress Rome" as irresponsible or cowardly, it should be noted that the resources saved by changing from an imperialist to a seemingly isolationist strategy were used to help solve Rome's domestic problems. Hadrian knew that the best way to regain the solid support of the Roman people was to abandon open-ended imperial involvements and take actions to solve internal problems that had been caused or exacerbated by those involvements. Under the circumstances, it was a constructive reaction to military failure.

There is another fact about the hundred years initiated by Hadrian, known as the era of the Antonine Emperors, that should be mentioned. According to Gibbon, the Antonine period was the happiest era ever known to the world. On close examination, however, we find that although social problems were attended to and there was the equivalent of urban renewal as well as extensive public works, there is no evidence of new ideas during this period—not one vital literary work, no art that was not borrowed from an earlier period or another country, and no technological progress. It was a century of complacent happiness, of unequaled financial prosperity, and finally of monumental dullness. In these days when conventional wisdom holds that the greatest good for the greatest number depends on increasing the size of the economic pie so that everyone can have a bigger slice I dare not suggest that Rome's very success in solving the GNP/employment problem was the cause of this atrophy in the arts, literature, and ideas. There may very well be some connection between the Antonine prosperity, the ways the Romans chose to enjoy their prosperity, their acceptance of the institution of slavery, and their indifference to a government that, through its policy of benevolent despotism, enabled the citizens to avoid being concerned with their nation's real problems and the ensuing decline and fall of the Roman Empire. . . . I don't know, but I do know that if we knew the real meaning of the Roman peoples' readiness during the Antonine period to accept a totalitarian regime for the sake of the prospect of personal safety and the maintenance of their personal wealth we should be able to find a formula of some value for our own future.

Returning to our examination of the phenomenon of military failure, the response of Spain to its catastrophic involvement in the war in the Netherlands during the sixteenth century is strikingly similar in its conditions and motivations, to the U.S. involvement in Vietnam.

In the 1500s Spain was the dominant power in Europe. Under Charles V (1500–58), who was King of Spain (1516–56) and Emperor of the Holy Roman Empire (1519–56), and his son, Philip II (1527–98), Spain pursued a policy of ideological or religious imperialism that sought the unification of Christendom in the Catholic faith under Spanish leadership and the preservation of Catholic Christendom, by force if necessary, against Protestant attack or subversion.

Spain's war in the Netherlands was a direct result of her anti-Protestantism policy and her assumption that she must have direct control over the internal affairs of the Dutch people. On the one hand, Spanish anti-Protestantism—much like America's post-World War II anti-Communism—was used to portray the war as a crusade against heresy and the forces of Satan, which was helpful in playing on the fears and superstitions of the Spanish people but made acknowledging the fact of Spain's subsequent military failure immeasurably more difficult because the forces of "right" *had* to appear to succeed because God was on their side. On the other hand, Spain's commitment to the Netherlands was based less on a real need to become directly involved in Dutch domestic affairs in order to honor that commitment than on a mistaken notion about the greater efficiency of Spanish rule.

The Netherlands fell to Charles V by inheritance from his father, Philip of Castile (House of Burgundy), without opposition. The Dutch people and aristocracy were willing to accept Charles as their sovereign just as they had accepted his father. They were also fully capable of managing the responsibilities of local government and citizenship. However, Charles V was led to believe that they needed the greater "civilizing" influence of direct Spanish rule in order to root out Protestantism and Protestants. Thus, instead of requiring the Dutch to rid themselves of the Protestant heresy, he sent his own experts in religious "pacification" to govern the country and to advise the Dutch leaders about how to promote the "true faith."

Philip II, in attempting to continue his father's policies, was motivated as much by his own personal religious fervor and ambition to be designated Holy Roman Emperor as by a belief in the holiness of Spain's national mission. He was a genuine imperialist. But by the late 1560s Spanish control was deteriorating. Protestants were springing up where there had been none before and the Dutch were becoming much less receptive to their Spanish "advisers." In short, an insurrection was brewing, if not already underway. Opinion was divided in Philip's court over how to deal with the rebels. The regent, Margaret of Parma, was in favor of a policy designed to "win the hearts and minds" of the rebels and re-educate them to the eternal truths of the Catholic Church. The Duke of Alba, who had recently returned to Spain after a distinguished military career in Germany and Italy, advocated the equivalent of "search and destroy." The argument between the hawks and doves waxed, waned, and finally waxed, resulting in Margaret's resignation and her replacement by the Duke of Alba, who was also named governor general of the Netherlands, in which role he proceeded to crush Dutch attempts to gain religious toleration and political self-government. In 1567 Alba led Spain's elite force of *tercios* on a massive campaign of "reconquest" in order to force the Dutch into total subjugation and to eliminate once and for all any vestiges of Protestantism.

Alba's "successes" were phenomenal. The special court he set up at Brussels, popularly known as the Court of Blood, executed some eighteen thousand persons for "crimes against God and Philip," and the estates and assets of those executed were confiscated to help defray the cost of the war and pay Alba's army. But because these funds were not enough to cover the costs, Alba was forced to increase taxes, which further exacerbated relations between the "loyal" Dutch Catholics and their Spanish masters. Several cities rebelled, only to be punished by Alba with much bloodshed. He kept the "peace" the only way he knew, but after six years it was obvious to Philip and the Spanish court that Alba was creating more problems than he solved, both in the Netherlands and in Spain. For example, when Alba took command in the Netherlands it did not have an army and there was no organized opposition to Spanish rule; by 1573 the Dutch had forged a national guerrilla organization that was more than a match for the better-armed and equipped *tercios* in the water-seamed countryside of the northern Netherlands, and the persecution and murder of Protestants had embroiled Spain in additional conflicts with England and the Huguenots of France. The irony of Alba's "success" as he attempted to pursue the Dutch guerrillas into the marshes is that his enemies in Philip's court were able to force his resignation on the grounds that his unwarranted diversion of scarce military resources against an "inferior" enemy had compromised the royalist cause of Spain in more important areas. Alba was hoist with his own petard, in that he had denigrated the Dutch guerrillas in terms of their assumed moral and physical inferiority.

Unfortunately, Philip's acceptance of Alba's resignation in 1573 did not signal the end of Spain's agony in the Netherlands nor that of the Dutch people. The war went on; Philip could neither win it nor end it. The superior military techniques of the Spaniards were costly and ineffective in a guerrilla-war environment and each attempt to coerce the Dutch population, both Catholic and Protestant, resulted in greater support for both the guerrillas' political cause and their recruitment program. In Spain itself, the heavy taxation needed for the war produced grave social discontent because the burden fell on the poor rather than the rich. The social fabric of Spain was thoroughly rent by the war in the Netherlands. There were riots, scandals in the government and army, increases in crime and banditry, rejection of secular and religious moral values, youthful disillusionment with historically acceptable social goals, and the beginning of drug addiction as a social problem. (According to some historians, the drug problem in sixteenth-century Spain was not due to the Netherlands war, but rather to Spanish soldiers who had picked up the peyote/mescaline habit in the New World and who on their way to the Netherlands by way of Spain passed their habit on to the civilian society.)

By the 1590s it was perfectly clear to Philip and his ministers that they had to get out of the Netherlands, but Philip was in no way ready to be the first Spanish emperor to preside over a Spanish defeat, or, in our terms, military failure. His problem was made doubly difficult because, in addition to admitting that Spain could not defeat the Dutch guerrillas, he had to acknowledge the "unacknowledgeable"—the de facto legitimacy and equality of the Protestant rebels. He could do neither. At the time of his death in 1598, after an abortive attempt to end direct Spanish military intervention by a policy of "Netherlandization" and substituting foreign mercenaries for Spanish troops—and after granting "independence" to the Netherlands under the rule of his daughter, Isabel Clara Eugenia, and her husband, Archduke Albert—Philip II left his son, Philip III, with an even more intractable situation.

Philip III had no new plan for ending the war. From his point of view it mattered not that Spain was bankrupt, that the burden of taxation to support the war was destroying Spanish society, and that each of Spain's social problems was rapidly getting beyond the point of solution. All that mattered was that the war had to go on to a successful conclusion. And so it did, for ten more years, concluding only after "success" was redefined outside of the objectives under which Spain went to war in the first place. The difference between Philip III's years in the Netherlands and those of his father and grandfather was the ability of his commanders to achieve some notable successes in the field against the Dutch, such as the three-year siege and capture of Ostend in 1604. Even so, these victories were due more to the fact that by that time the war had become more conventional than to any significant improvement in Spain's combat effectiveness against the Dutch. That is, in general terms, a conventional army with greater firepower, better organization, and more experience in regular warfare can be expected to win a conventional battle more than a less experienced, less well-equipped, newly created conventional army. Nevertheless, in spite of the fact that the Dutch army had evolved out of a loose guerrilla organization and was inferior to the Spanish armies in terms of equipment and firepower, it was not defeated in all the conventional battles fought in the war's late stages. But neither the Dutch nor Spanish victories of that period were militarily conclusive; neither could defeat the other thoroughly enough to be able to claim victory and make the claim stick. Nonetheless, out of this record of alternating victory and defeat the Spanish stumbled on a face-saving device to end the war: the use of a truce instead of a peace settlement.

The resolution of "Philip's Paradox"—that is, the physical impossibility for Spain's forces to win decisively and the political impossibility for them to admit defeat—is a good example of how quickly and in what direction a war-weary people can turn their hostilities in the face of a military failure. In 1607, acting on the advice of his "Special Assistant for National Security," the Duke of Lerma, Philip ordered his commander in the Netherlands, Spinola, to end the war in such a way that it would appear he was acting out of a deep sense of compassion toward the common people of the Netherlands and Spain who had suffered so long. Philip's camouflaged compassion worked where all of the massed firepower of Spain's *tercios* had failed, but not until after two years of the most difficult negotiations ever carried out to end any war.

The negotiations were finally concluded by avoiding what had become the principal issue of the conflict: the recognition of the Netherlands' independence. Although the religious issue continued to be cited by the Church hierarchy as the moral justification for continuing the war, it had long since become incidental to the question of Dutch independence. Spain could not extend formal recognition and independence to the Netherlands because of domestic pressures and the Dutch could not, or would not, settle for less. Philip ordered Spinola to strike a balance between these two apparently irreconcilable extremes and end the war, in the words of Correlli Barnett, "without seeming to desire it." This Spinola did by concluding the Twelve Years' Truce of 1609, which finessed the issue of recognition/independence and initiated the era of "partition" politics. The truce was sold to Spain's hawks and religious birds of prey as an act of compassion reluctantly agreed to by Philip to give the people of both countries a chance to recover from the ravages of war while a final political solution favorable to Spain was worked out. The supposedly temporary truce was never really broken, and the partition of the Netherlands—represented today by Belgium and Holland—became a permanent fact of Spain's political life. Once the fighting was stopped, the division of the Netherlands and the de facto recognition of its independence became a much less compelling domestic political issue. The only solace to Spanish imperialist and religious ideologues after forty years of inconclusive warfare and successive stages of military failure was that the southern Netherlands remained Catholic, as it had all along.

Finally, it should be noted that the public was distracted from Philip's seeming "softness on Protestantism"—and from awareness of Spain's military failure—by the Spanish army's domestic "search and destroy" mission against a racial minority, the Moriscos, Christians of Moorish descent who lived in Spain. In 1609 they numbered approximately 300,000, part of the successful imperial legacy left by Ferdinand and Isabella after their defeat of the Moors in an exceptionally bloody, and truly religious, war a hundred years earlier. This victory over the Moors, who had occupied Spain since the 700s, is the high point of Spanish military accomplishment. Ferdinand and Isabella had expelled great numbers of Moors, but those who had converted to Christianity, or were willing to, had been allowed to stay in Spain.

The "War Against the Moriscos" was launched on the very day the Twelve Years' Truce was signed, when Philip decreed that all Moriscos be expelled from Spain. There is no need to dwell on the methods, rationalizations, and subterfuges the Spaniards used to accomplish this, nor on the variety of legal ruses and psychological perversions used to allow a favored few to remain, such as designating them "honorary Castilians." The end result was that all but twenty-five thousand of the Moriscos were forcibly deported to North Africa, and their property was expropriated to declare a Netherlands War "bonus" and to pay off, or otherwise quiet, those who might have been inclined to question and oppose Philip's right to remain on the throne. The obvious racial implications of the white-skinned Spanish Castilians expelling the Moriscos, who by and large were black or of mixed blood, should not be overlooked because it shows how quickly seemingly nonracial tensions can break up an apparently peaceful integrated multiracial society.

Finally, although there is no provable link between Spain's military failure in the Netherlands, her antisocial domestic response, and her almost uninterrupted subsequent decline and fall as a major power, this historical record should give us cause to pause because it illustrates the difficulty and hazards of abandoning a forward strategy even under an absolute monarchy. It shows that although a military failure can provide the opportunity to change a bad policy, there is no automatic assurance that the next policy will be a good one, or even an improvement, or that if the next policy fails there will be a chance for another.

With an eye on the problem of how a nation should go about selecting a better "next" policy following a military failure, and inferentially improving the odds over getting a chance to continue to select policies in the search for the "best" one, let us turn to an examination of how Great Britain has coped with military failure in its overseas imperial wars.

The British experience with military failure, beginning in the fifteenth century with Henry V's abortive attempt to defend England's claim to sit *in absentia* on the French throne, through the American Revolution in the eighteenth century, to the Irish Rebellion in the twentieth, illustrates the difficulties faced even by a democratic society in coping with this phenomenon and its aftereffects.

In the case of Henry V's campaign in France, Britain early and easily acquired large pieces of territory, all of which had to be garrisoned by British troops. The results were similar to those experienced by Emperor Trajan in the Near East: capture of key terrain, occupation, thinning down of assault forces to defend newly created exterior lines of communications, a local population made hostile by the occupation, the emergence of a guerrilla force, beginnings of a guerrilla war, an expansion of the occupation force and its absorption of the "counterguerrilla" mission, and so on. For those who think the cycle can be broken by making an effort to alter one or more of its elements, it should be noted as a general proposition that the only apparent exception to this process is when the foreign occupation is the result of a "peaceful" conquest following a legitimate purchase, marriage between two royal houses, or a political annexation that leaves the local government intact. Because the cycle described in this case was apparent to those expected to pay for Henry V's war in

France—the members of Parliament and English royalty—a political backlash of sorts emerged in opposition to the war.

England had the usual accompanying problems of domestic discontent: high taxes and public dissatisfaction with a government that had no time, energy, or resources left over from the war to meet the needs of the people. In this instance two other problems emerged—massive military insubordination and a breakdown in law and order. The insubordination was due to a widespread belief on the part of the British forces that they had been sold out by politicians and even by their king, and took the form of refusing to acknowledge and carry out orders. A striking example of how military insubordination can upset "secret" political discussion to end a war is seen in the refusal of the English commanders in the field to yield the French province of Maine to the French even though Henry VI had agreed to its cession as part of the overall peace package. Their refusal to give up territory they and their forces had captured at great human cost for a political objective they did not share can be understood, but it infuriated the politicians, who—then as now—retain the right to redefine those objectives in midstream.

This insubordination in France and England spread like wild fire, culminating in Jack Cade's rebellion in 1450, which used as its rallying point an unconfirmed rumor that the politicians had sold out the British forces before the final English defeat in Normandy at Formigny earlier in the year by giving the English battle plan to the French, thereby sabotaging the delivery of supplies and reinforcements. Thus, five hundred years before World War I, the "stab in the back" tactic was used by a frustrated military establishment in a successful attempt to manipulate the politicians. The upshot of these charges and counter-charges was that the military was able to get off the hook for their poor showing in the so-called Hundred Years' War by shifting the blame to the civilian leaders who had initiated the war. In an effort to appease the military, Henry VI executed his chief minister, the Earl of Suffolk, on charges of general incompetence and poor judgment, which did appease them, but only barely. So Henry acted to diminish their potential power by the only sure method available to any ruling politician: he reduced the size of the armed forces. He was successful in that the military became less of a political concern, but the Hundred Years' War veterans who had been demobilized to defuse the political situation then became part of England's social problem. They carried over into civilian life the habits—such as raping, looting, and pillaging—and attitudes engendered by the fighting in France, which intensified and accelerated the breakdown of law and order in England following the Hundred Years' War and provided the "everyone does it" rationalization for the brutal violence in the internecine factional Wars of the Roses between 1455 and 1485.

This illustrates another of the consequences of military failure. Victorious soldiers come home happy to be alive and looking forward to their future. Defeated soldiers come home disconsolate and cautious about their personal future, but if they have fought well at least their honor is left intact. Soldiers who have been part of a military failure, however, come home like thieves in the night, social outcasts without even the solace of knowing theirs was an honorable defeat. In fifteenth-century England, the soldiers demobilized for political reasons did not feel bound by the mores, taboos, or laws of England and vented their recriminations and hatreds on a system that had used them and then cast them aside. They became a law unto themselves, and a very disruptive element in English civilian life.

Turning to the British experience in America during the Revolutionary War, we will see that military failure does not automatically have to result in social disorder. The American Revolution, from the British point of view, can properly be classified as the wrong war at the wrong time and indubitably in the wrong place.

Before discussing the political and social aspects of the British military failure in America, we should mention two basic factors that aggravated Britain's problems.

One was that the British thought their troops could be fed primarily on the output of American agriculture, a blooper of classical proportions. To begin with, the Americans had barely enough to sustain their own population, much less foreign troops. Further, the British were misinformed about the loyalty of the American public, feeling that only a dissident minority was anti-British and that the majority of colonists would support them. They weren't prepared for the general hostility they met, which was increased in the wake of the pillaging Hessian mercenaries the British brought in. And when the British finally realized their troops would have to be supplied from England, it was a case of too little and too late. Thus in addition to severe problems of getting supplies to the troops, they could not keep large contingents of men in the field at any given time.

The other was the organizational ineptitude displayed by the British war planners, who fought the war by whim and committee. They never appointed a single war chief to coordinate strategy, and throughout the war were hampered by interdepartmental suspicion and jealousy. Edward E. Curtis, in *The British Army in the American Revolution,* concludes, "The Admiralty, the Treasury, and the Colonial Office bickered perpetually. And the army itself was administered by a series of 'Boards,' each dealing with some more or less separate aspect of army affairs, . . . characterized by a muddle of overlapping, duplication, and decentralization of authority, which was painfully apparent in peacetime, but became in a war of the American order a serious obstacle to the success of British arms."

These difficulties—one physical, the other conceptual and organizational—did not cause the British military failure in America, but they provided General Washington with balancing advantages that, given the essential weakness of his army and the lack of American popular support for the revolution, he otherwise would not have had. One historian of the revolutionary period contends that Washington's only real problem was to keep his army in the field until the British defeated themselves. To understand this British military failure we should remember that it was a war embarked on in supposed pursuit—not defense—of the Principle of the Crown and Parliament's supremacy, a principle, one might add, that initially was not in question in America. But because George III and Lord North believed it was, they acted on the fallacious idea that free men would willingly accept royal discrimination in its application.

In assessing the British performance in the American Revolution it is important to be aware of the trends of public opinion in England and their influence on the course of the war. At the beginning, in 1775, English support of the Crown's stated cause was lukewarm, and in areas from which many of the colonists had migrated it was warmly sympathetic to the American cause. When the French intervened on behalf of the colonists, it evoked a greater sense of national support and unity in the English public, although this was more anti-French than it was anti-American. This lack of public support for the war in the early stages and the subsequent intervention of the French affected the British armed forces in quite specific ways.

As was also the case with the U.S. involvement in Vietnam, when the American Revolution broke out, both the British Army and Navy had to be built up to meet the emergency, but because of the indifference and opposition to the war in the classes from which recruits were normally drawn, voluntary recruitment broke down completely. Moreover, opposition to the war also had an effect on the active serving establishment, as revealed by the disaffection of a set of key officers who believed that they were being improperly called upon to suppress a legitimate rebellion. The Commander in Chief of the British Army, Lord Amherst, refused to take command in the field in America, an action that would be akin to General Westmoreland telling President Johnson, "Hell no, I won't go!" Scores of less important officers also refused to go, despite the effect this would have on their careers.* Even Lord Howe, who did take command of British forces in America, went most reluctantly, making clear that his mission was not victory but peace. It is interesting to note, in this connection, that the British Army has always been, with the exception of World Wars I and II, a long-service force based on voluntary enlistment and officered by men drawn from the propertied classes. Thus, the so-called all-volunteer army is not necessarily

---

* G. O. Trevelyan, *The American Revolution,* McKay, New York, 1964, Vol. III, p. 202.

consistent with the theory of the "passive military instrument."

The disaffection of these officers was not widespread enough to cause George III to abandon the war, but it did have an influence well out of proportion to the numbers involved in that it forced the Crown to adopt the worst possible kinds of recruiting practices in an ideologically oriented war—the use of "press gangs" to provide sailors for the English navy and the hiring of foreign mercenaries to fill the ranks of the army in America. There is no need to dwell unduly on the savage methods of the press gangs, but their use had an incalculable effect on England's seagoing commerce. Whole crews of merchant ships were captured by the pressmen and turned over to the Royal Navy, which may have solved one problem but created others of even greater significance. Correspondingly, the use of foreign mercenaries not only failed to solve the military manpower needs of the British Army but can be seen as the proximate cause of the British military failure in the American Revolution.

Let us look at the two-stage utilization of mercenaries in the American Revolution. In the first stage, as already mentioned, the shortage of volunteers forced the Crown to hire the so-called Hessians, who were nothing more than innocent German peasants literally sold by German nobles to the British. Their performance in the revolution is without any real military significance, either pro or con. They were poorly equipped by British army standards and incredibly badly led by British officers who treated them like subhumans and who, because of the language barrier, were unable to do little more than bellow to make themselves and their orders understood. But the Hessians' "foreignness" set them apart and that, coupled with their ostensible military role, provoked a xenophobic reaction from the American colonists. From xenophobia it was easy to picture the British effort in America as an "invasion" by a foreign power and, as we have seen in Vietnam and elsewhere, this destroyed any sympathy for Britain's aims both at home and in the beleaguered colonies. Moreover, the valid argument was forced upon those Americans who perceived their militant opposition to the Crown as a legitimate defense of the honored Whig principle of "no taxation without representation," rather than an attempt to achieve American independence, that if the English were willing to use German mercenaries, there was no moral reason why the colonists should not use French assistance if they could get it. Another effect of "internationalizing" a local war is that the uncommitted middle, or those who tend to remain morally neutral in the face of militant protest for principle, are much more likely to become involved—"radicalized"—if an outside foreign element is used to solve the argument, and this also happened in the case of the American Revolution.

In the second stage, as part of British harassment—or, in modern-day terms, their "pacification program"—of the colonists, a "counterguerrilla" operation was launched on the frontier, using Indians who were paid off with whiskey and beads for killing the American Revolution's equivalent of Vietcong sympathizers. The results of this "Phoenix program" were predictable: decent Englishmen of all political persuasions were ashamed, and the Americans were made angry, bitter, and disillusioned.

Granted the resources of the times, the American Revolution was perhaps beyond the technical capacity and resources of England to win; however, the fact that half the English people had no desire to see it won and felt genuine disgust at Britain's use of Hessians and Indians is a vital element in causing Britain's military failure. Nevertheless, in spite of the preponderant amount of contrary psychological and physical evidence, the British government remained confident that it would achieve ultimate victory.

The principal reasons for this persistent optimism on the part of George III and his ministers are common enough to the phenomenon of military failure to merit mention: (1) an assumed inferiority on the part of the opposition's forces; * (2) an

---

* Consider, for example, Lord Germaine's appreciation of the American revolutionary forces as late as spring 1781, when he said, "So contemptible is the rebel force in all parts, and so vast is our superiority everywhere, that no resistance on their part is to be apprehended that can materially obstruct the progress of the King's arms in the speedy repression of the rebellion." William Lecky, *History of England*, AMS Press, New Work, 1892, Vol. IV, p. 392. The same outlook is reflected even more tersely in the

assumed indifference on the part of the indigenous population during a counterrevolutionary campaign carried out by *nonlocal* forces; and (3) that peace proposals offering the rebels what they already have achieved, or are likely to achieve by force in the foreseeable future, are concessions. None of these reasons is particularly valid, but then neither are the reasons for starting a war to spread an ideological principle, or to force its acceptance by the population of a distant nation or region. This conclusion rests on the obvious fact that there is a fundamental difference between a social upheaval and a nationalist rebellion: the former is almost always broadly based at the start and the latter rarely is.

There are two other features about the aftermath of the American Revolution that tell us something about what may happen when a democratic government liquidates a military failure. First, by the time Cornwallis surrendered to Washington at Yorktown in October 1781 the social ferment in England, which had come from deeper causes than the war itself, had boiled over. The war had served to accelerate the process of social change by focusing public attention on the failure of the ancient and corrupt structure of the British state to win a war they treated too lightly, entered into wrongly, and could not prevent from widening from a local domestic quarrel into a general war. The social change was manifested as much by the beginnings of the Industrial Revolution as by new ideas about political freedom and representative government. Forces wanting social reform united to bring the futile war to an end and to address domestic problems that had been deferred because of the war.

Second, the new government of Rockingham Whigs, which came to power early in 1782 and which had been elected on a policy of ending the war, moved too quickly and gave up too much in fulfillment of their campaign pledge. The British who still held Charleston, South Carolina; New York; Rhode Island; and Penobscot, Maine, were not imperiled in any way by the sur-

words of General William C. Westmoreland during his tenure as commander of American forces in Vietnam: "We're smarter [than the Vietnamese Communists] . . . and we've got more guts." *Army Digest,* February 1967, p. 41, quoting General Westmoreland.

render at Yorktown, but the British government made no effort to trade its control of these places for guarantees of the safety and property rights of American "loyalists" who had supported them throughout the war. Amid talk about bloodbaths, the British simply packed up and "got out of America," leaving their former supporters to fend for themselves. Although the predicted blood-bath did not materialize, the British found out that their precipitate departure had helped to unify America in its opposition to England more than it might have been if some semblance of concern had been manifested about the "loyalists." In fairness to the new English government, it must be noted that it—especially the younger Pitt, who became Prime Minister in 1783—faced up to their domestic problems, brought the English people together, and led Great Britain to a pre-eminent postwar position as a democratic society based upon the principles of constitutional government.

But Great Britain's successful experience in overcoming her military failure in the American Revolution did not provide her leaders with the wisdom to avoid a similar experience in Ireland in the twentieth century. The Ireland experience is of recent enough vintage—and so well illustrates the potential of the so-called war of national liberation to cause a major power's military failure—that it merits close consideration as a case study of the phenomenon, especially since it has not yet received the careful consideration it so richly deserves.

FOUR

Military Failure: Ireland, 1916-22

> "By intensity of hatred nations create in themselves the character they imagine in their enemies. Hence it is that all passionate conflicts result in the interchange of characteristics."
>
> —George William Russell

IRELAND has always been a thorn in the British Crown, and for nearly three hundred years its northeast corner has been an exceptionally trying barb. There is no need to review the entire history of Ireland, but it is necessary to take a fairly close look at selected events in the conflict in the 1916–22 period to get some sense of the struggle waged for control of the Irish nation, which produced a classical military failure for England. The political origin of the past fifty years of the Irish struggle against English rule is as ironic as anything in the history of military failure because it is based on the mistaken notion that an outside power can maintain its rule and control over a portion of a previously independent sovereign nation after the fact of a military failure. Under these circumstances, partition is no more a permanent solution to the problem of nation-state political relationships than the colonial conquest that precedes it.*

* For example, even today in Northern Ireland, the people who remain opposed to partition—although not necessarily to commonwealth status within the United Kingdom—refuse to accept the official name and call it the "Six Counties." On the other hand, the northern Unionists continue to call the area by its historic name, Ulster, which falsely equates the six counties of Northern Ireland with the nine of Ulster. And finally those in the north and south who see the English presence in Northern Ireland as

The political and military strategy and tactics developed and carried out by the Sinn Fein/IRA * during the 1916–22 period were designed to achieve one primary goal: to make the English administration of Ireland impossible. They were based on valid principles of insurrectional warfare that exploited or served to create favorable conditions for the accomplishment of this goal and its related objective, Ireland's political independence.

Implicit in their particular strategy was the absolute necessity for correct organization of the guerrilla force. For example, the IRA was kept small in relation to the total number of men who wanted to join, and the number of volunteers in any one action was never allowed to exceed two hundred, because a tightly knit insurrectionary organization working to a detailed plan against regular troops has a much greater chance of success than the classic liberation type of insurrectionary army. The basic IRA unit was a company consisting of seventy-six to a hundred men, recruited and based locally.

In the command and control of these companies the IRA leadership had one advantage not usually available to the leaders of a nationalist-oriented insurrection—a guerrilla organization with a long tradition of unhesitating obedience to orders and secrecy in planning its operations. This was because the selection of IRA leaders was based upon the "consent of the led" and because the IRA grew out of the Irish Republican Brotherhood (IRB), whose members had been required to swear the following oath: "In the presence of God, I, ———, do solemnly swear that I will do my utmost to establish the National Independence of Ireland; that I will bear true faith and allegiance to the Supreme Council of the Irish Republican Brotherhood and Govern-

one of an occupying power call it simply "the North." The rest of Ireland also has its share of titles, all of which are in use today and which reflect the underlying reality of the Irish people's attitudes toward the incompleteness of the Irish rebellion. These titles include: the Free State, Eire (Gaelic for Ireland), the Twenty-six Counties, Southern Ireland (or the South), and the Republic of Ireland or simply "the Republic."

* Sinn Fein (Ourselves Alone) is the Irish republican political party and organization that had as its prime goal the complete severance of all ties with Britain and the unity of all Ireland. The IRA, of course, is the Irish Republican Army.

ment of the Irish Republic; that I will implicitly obey the Constitution of the Irish Republican Brotherhood, and all my superior officers; and preserve inviolable the secrets of the organization. So help me God!"

At the beginning of 1919 when the Dail was constituted by the Sinn Fein as the National Assembly of Ireland—albeit as an extralegal rump government—the individual IRB volunteer's oath became an oath of allegiance to the Dail and the IRB was renamed the IRA. In the selection of IRA leaders, company officers were elected by their men and higher regimental officers by the company commanders. These elections had to be ratified by the IRA central headquarters.

The IRA struck the ideal balance between centralized control over its individual companies and provision for the flexibility and freedom of action they needed in order to carry out their assigned missions. IRA actions on a major scale were the result of a general plan and each of these actions was specifically ordered by the IRA central headquarters. However, the details about how to actually carry out the major actions were developed by the local companies, which also were allowed autonomy in selecting, planning, and executing small-scale attacks against targets of opportunity and those developed by their own local intelligence operations, as long as these smaller attacks could be carried out over a long term and on a rising scale.

The underlying principles involved in applying the IRA's strategy and tactics suggest that the only method by which a small nation or a national, religious, or ideological group can hope to rid itself of an occupying power is by making the occupation uneconomical and politically unacceptable to those who must pay for it and psychologically, if not physically, untenable for those who actually carry out the occupation. Close analysis of the British Army's performance in Ireland shows that it could not be defeated by IRA forces in open and extended battle, but the IRA was able to convince many British military leaders that it was better to leave Ireland rather than suffer the loss of public respect and control over their troops as the acts of brutality common to guerrilla war—such as the torture of prisoners without regard to age, sex, or condition of capture—that their troops had been carrying out became known to the general public in England.

IRA guerrilla warfare techniques were advanced by the most ruthless and spartan methods. The IRA deliberately sabotaged the economy of Ireland, thereby increasing the British Army's occupation costs. It forced the people of Ireland to ostracize both the police and the British Army so that any friendly contact was impossible. Simultaneously the Sinn Fein used political pressures to reinforce IRA activities. They mobilized world opinion in support of the Irish Republican cause, especially among Americans of Irish extraction, and they made an effective appeal to the social conscience of such English intellectual leaders as George Bernard Shaw and Sidney and Beatrice Webb. But the final persuader was the IRA itself, which broke the English civil administration of Ireland by attacking its instruments, forcing their replacement by military ones that were much less efficient, and then carefully escalating the war on a planned basis to a point and under conditions whereby a military failure was finally acknowledged and accepted by England's political leaders.

The importance of leadership to the successful execution of the Sinn Fein/IRA's strategy and tactics is best measured by the effectiveness and manner in which its leaders controlled and directed their forces against those of the British. Occasionally military failure occurs almost in spite of the rebel leadership. As a general proposition we can say that a military failure is more likely to occur if the rebel leadership is good and is able to bring about political acceptance of failure before the status quo military forces are allowed to bring full military power to bear against the rebels. In the case of Ireland, the character of the rebel leadership is fully revealed in the career of the man who conceptualized, argued for, and directed the war's militant strategy—Michael Collins, the "Big Fellow." *

In Michael Collins' career we have proof of the fact that in any creative endeavor demanding truly independent innovative

---

* See Piaras Beaslai, *Life of Michael Collins*, Vols. I & II, for a sympathetic biography of Collins the *political* leader.

action, there is no accounting for men of genius. The son of a Clonakilty farmer, Collins had only enough education to qualify as a boy clerk in London's Government Post Office, yet he was to emerge as the man to whom the citizen soldiers in the IRA looked for leadership, guidance, and action. He gave them all three. Unfortunately for Ireland, his career was short-lived, for he was killed in action at the age of thirty-two by his former IRA comrades-in-arms during the Irish Civil War of 1922–23, when pro-treaty and anti-treaty forces fought an even fiercer war than the Anglo-Irish war that preceded it.

Michael Collins' career explains a great deal about the phenomenon of military failure in that it shows how a gifted rebel leader, with only a small force, can create the conditions necessary to bring about the status quo power's downfall. Many have aspired the revolutionary's role, but few have succeeded. Collins was one of the few.

As his biographers have pointed out, Collins had a strong, charismatic personality and was the strictest of disciplinarians, dealing harshly with those who failed to carry out their missions or made excuses for poor showings. These qualities, in addition to his ability to remain unremittingly committed to the rebel cause, to make life-and-death decisions boldly, and—in spite of his lack of formal military training and his mercurial temperament—to give meticulous attention to the thorny details of fighting a guerrilla war, go a long way toward explaining why his leadership was so crucial. But the overriding factor was that his involvement was more personal than political, more "Irish" than ideological.

Always with the fact of Collins' leadership in mind, we will examine the events of the Irish rebellion insofar as they pertain to the phenomenon of military failure.

The first event was the 1916 "Easter Rising" in Dublin, which broke a two-century history of Irish revolutionary movements that had always ended in disaster, although it too was technically a failure. The rebels employed all the wrong tactics, but out of their costly mistakes and errors of judgment there emerged the conditions for the ultimate success of their cause, the unity of Ireland free from English control. This is because, in revolutionary strategy, it is possible to use an unsuccessful insurrection as means to create, or enhance, the social, political, or economic conditions required to force a military failure upon the status quo forces. In this case, the principle worked in that the methods the British forces used to suppress the Easter Rising changed Irish public opinion toward the rebel cause from one of general indifference to one of popular support.

Because the rebel leaders were willing to sacrifice their own lives in the execution of their plan they were able to force the English to use the British Army's full firepower to liquidate the rebellion. The English authorities, using arguments similar to those of American authorities during the 1968 Tet Offensive, justified their use of point-blank artillery fire to clear built-up areas defended by the Irish rebels on the grounds that it would speed up a slow and expensive process and thereby minimize the *total* number of casualties. Although the argument is technically correct and highly persuasive from a "cost-effective" standpoint, it is totally irrelevant in a war with a high ideological content. Also, the authorization by the English government for the British Army Commander in Ireland, General Sir John Maxwell, under the provisions of martial law, to summarily execute those he believed to be the instigators and leaders of the rebellion played into the hands of the rebels, who were thus able to construct a brand-new martyrology, an essential feature of their revolutionary strategy.

This form of martyrology is based on the further principle that if a status quo government takes only a few lives in exercising its arbitrary authority under emergency conditions, rather than "wiping out the rebels to the last man," there is a strong likelihood that the rebellion will continue to grow stronger in succeeding periods. The principle is best illustrated by comparing the "body counts" of the Easter Rising with those of the Paris Commune of 1871 and the subsequent evolution of the respective revolutionary movements.

In the Easter Rising fifty-six rebels and one hundred thirty

English were killed. There were more than thirty-five hundred prisoners, nearly three times as many as there had been actual insurgents during Easter Week. Of these, seventeen hundred were deported to England, seventy-three were sentenced to penal servitude and six to imprisonment at hard labor, and ninety-seven were condemned to death.* But due to public outrage in England and the United States, the executions were halted after only fifteen of the rebels were shot. In Paris, on the other hand, according to Jellinek in *The Paris Commune of 1871*, a total of more than fifty thousand were killed in the assault on Paris and the massacre that followed, died in prison, or were jailed or deported. The mass killings of prisoners was ruthless. Outside of Paris, for example, Jellinek estimates that nineteen hundred were shot at La Roquette and four hundred at Marzas in a two-day period.

In France, as a result of the extreme punitive measures taken by the French forces loyal to President Thiers against the Communards, the movement was effectively destroyed, and the Third Republic, proclaimed in 1870, lasted until the Nazi occupation in 1940. The point, of course, is that not only were *all* the actual Communard leaders and most of its potential leaders killed, but that enough rank-and-file rebels were killed to deter sympathizers from undertaking a similar movement in the future. Summary punishment may not be an effective deterrent to criminal acts, but it proved its worth in France as a deterrent to potentially violent rebellious political activity.† In Ireland the

---

* MacArdle, Dorothy, *The Irish Republic: A Documented Chronicle of the Anglo-Irish Conflict and the Partitioning of Ireland with a Detailed Account of the Period 1916–23*, Farrar, Strauss & Giroux, New York, 1965, p. 117. See also, *Royal Commission on the Rebellion in Ireland: Evidence and Documents*, London, 1916.

† Lest the reader leap to an unwarranted conclusion that mass reprisal is a valid way to counter a revolution or an insurgency, it should be borne in mind that although such a method may be temporarily successful it sows the seeds of its own destruction because a people inhibited by fear of an arbitrary political force will sooner or later fail to respond positively to a genuine threat to their nation's existence. Witness the passive acquiescence of the overwhelming mass of the French people to the Nazi occupation of their country, a fact often obscured by idealizing the anti-Nazi exploits of the Macquis (French resistance fighters), which initially was

British Army's limited use of summary vengeance produced quite contrary results because the deaths of a handful of rebels evoked an overwhelming popular response of pity, admiration, and gratitude toward the martyred rebels and anger toward the English government. Encouragement of these attitudes, fanned by the tales of "British brutality," which was pictured as more and more barbarous with each telling, was crucially important to the rebels because in the past the Irish people had tended to be indifferent to the efforts of the Sinn Feiners to gain Ireland's independence. It is correct to say that the summary executions unified the Irish people in their opposition to English rule and elicited their *continued* active as well as passive support of the Sinn Fein's political and militant revolutionary activities.

The net result was to leave the IRA essentially intact and to give its remaining leaders a renewed sense of purpose and a compulsive need to avenge the deaths of their fallen comrades. In the case of Michael Collins, who was a company commander in the Easter Rising, the effect was sufficiently traumatic to motivate him to reach the heights of genius in the art of war, because he was present on the night of April 29, 1916, when his revolutionary mentor, the legendary Tom Clarke, was tortured and then executed by British officers.

To understand Tom Clarke and his influence on Michael Collins is to know the price of revolutionary leadership, and perhaps how it can only be paid. Clarke has been described as a slight man with gray hair and a worn gray face who looked older than his fifty-eight years, his pale blue eyes meek and inoffensive behind gold-rimmed spectacles. But he was part of the action, and his charisma was equally as great as Collins' was to become. He could and did lead a rebel force made up of men who literally could have ripped him in two. His strength of character and integrity in the cause of overthrowing English rule in Ireland was greater than that of his followers, and they knew it. An ex-convict who had spent fifteen years in English jails for his

composed almost exclusively of French Communist Party members and was only able to expand its membership after the Allies invaded Europe and the outcome of World War II was clear.

part in an Irish nationalist dynamite plot, Clarke had earned the right to lead the hard way.

Because Clarke was the ring leader of the Easter Rising, he was one of those singled out by the British for exemplary vengeance. Clarke and the other leaders were prepared to die for their beliefs, but because the British carried out Clarke's execution in a totally unprofessional way the rebels were able to turn his and the other deaths into a form of martyrology that they subsequently exploited very effectively.

On Saturday night, April 29, 1916, following the rebels' surrender earlier in the day, most of them were taken to the open-air Rotunda Gardens where they were held under armed guard by British soldiers until Sunday evening, when they were locked up in the Kilmainhan jail. A cold rain fell all Saturday night, during which time Tom Clarke was stripped naked, made to stand apart from his comrades, and was physically abused by a British officer. Clarke endured the abuse with the quiet abstraction he had learned in prison. This only infuriated and goaded the officer to greater excesses, but to no avail. Clarke was no mere "boy" in an English public school about to cry "enough" in response to an upper-classman's sadism and perversion.

The telling and retelling of this story throughout Ireland produced widespread popular support for the rebel cause. Unlike those who only heard about Clarke's torture after his execution, Michael Collins observed the indignities being inflicted on Clarke from a distance of about fifteen feet. Obviously the total effect upon Collins of seeing the physical debasement of his elderly mentor, leader, and friend cannot be measured. He did not forget what had been done to Tom Clarke; in 1920, when he was the IRA Director of Organization, he sent two of his most trusted followers to Gorey, where they found the officer who had abused Clarke and shot him down. Other evidence concerning the effect of Clarke's death on Michael Collins is indirect. However, generalizing from its influence on the Irish people and the IRA members' dedication to their revolutionary cause, there can be no doubt that it exerted a tremendous influence on how

Michael Collins acted to carry out the tasks and responsibilities of a revolutionary leader.

The second event in the Irish rebellion that pertains to the phenomenon of military failure is the Sinn Fein's use of the normal election process to give its rebellion a legitimacy it could not achieve by mere force of arms. In an explicit rejection of modern revolutionary conventional wisdom, which holds that a revolutionary party or force should boycott the normal election process, the Sinn Fein adopted unique election tactics to support their political strategy. They ran unpropertied young men for seats on the local government councils instead of supporting older property owners. Then, after the young men were elected they refused to recognize the authority of the local English Government Boards to order the local councils to collect taxes for the Crown. The tactic worked so well that many of the government services financed out of current local tax receipts were stopped. Thus, the young councilors were able to frustrate the English administration of Ireland at little risk to themselves because, under a quirk of English law, since they owned no property they could not be made personally liable for damages.

Although the Sinn Fein tactic of rigging the local councils was important in their overall strategy, their national or parliamentary election tactic was even more important. The Sinn Fein (Republican Party) made an all-out effort to elect their candidates to the English Parliament. The 1918 election results were remarkable. In the past, the Sinn Fein had virtually boycotted the electoral process, but in 1918 in the so-called "Khaki Election," it put up candidates in all but two constituencies, and out of the hundred and five members elected to the English Parliament from Ireland, seventy-three were Sinn Feiners. The Irish people had spoken. As a consequence, the Irish Parliamentary Party, which had been saying that the people of Ireland wanted nothing more than to be British subjects, was wiped out. Following this election, the Sinn Fein promptly organized its legally elected majority of Irish representatives to the English Parliament into a rump parliament called Dail Eireann. Although the Dail had no legal authority, it acted as if it did, and as a result the Irish people came to accept it as an alternative government, and their own. The English treated the Dail as little more than a debating society, but its formation, debates, and decrees provided the necessary political base from which to mount a guerrilla war.

Implicitly revealed in the Sinn Fein's successful use of the normal election process as part of their political strategy is the general principle, which I call "the last best chance to avoid a military failure." The principle, common to all military failures, holds that the dynamics of a war not directly involving a country's national interest are such that for a specific brief period there occurs a one-time most favorable opportunity to avoid the failure, after which the terms, conditions, and costs become less and less favorable until there is no possible way to avoid the failure. The regressive feature of the principle derives in part from the emotionalism and hardening of antagonisms that accompany so-called wars of national-ideological-religious liberation and in part from the practical political difficulties faced by any status quo authority if it gives up even a portion of its political power to "revolutionary" demands—that is, to demands it must treat as illegal. In order not to miss their last chance, the authorities must make quantitative and qualitative objective measurements and judgments at this point about the real and potential opposition. The task is difficult but not impossible, and does not imply surrender. However, few status quo governments have been able or willing to make an objective assessment of an insurgent's movement's demands, and even fewer to act—without substantial outside pressure—on the basis of such an assessment.

In the case of Ireland, England's last best chance occurred as a result of the December 1918 Parliamentary election's outcome. At this time, the Sinn Fein would have supported genuine home rule and dominion status for Ireland and would have remained in the English Commonwealth. But when it became apparent after the election that the real power in the English Parliament was not going to implement the Home Rule Bill already on the books, conditions for full-scale revolt were created.

The third event that pertains to the phenomenon of military failure is the Sinn Finn's use of an accepted instrument of international law—a declaration of war—to specify their objectives and the conditions under which they would oppose the English authority in Ireland. This time there was to be no abortive "Rising." As we have noted, the objective political conditions for a successful insurrection had been achieved partly by the actions of the English and partly by the Irish Republicans and, as a result, the Sinn Fein—using its alter-existence, the Dail Eireann—opted for war, guerrilla war. In so doing, the Dail, because it had provided Ireland with an alternative on-going system of government, was able to authorize the change of the Irish volunteers—the Irish Republican Brotherhood—into the Irish Republican Army, an accredited military force of a republic fighting to rid itself of an occupying power.

The gauntlet of war was thrown in the *An t-Oglach,* the IRA's newspaper, in the spring of 1919 when the Dail announced: "The state of war which is thus declared to exist, renders the national army the most important national service of the moment. It justifies Irish volunteers in treating the armed force of the enemy, whether soldiers or policemen, exactly as a national army would treat the members of an invading army. . . . Every volunteer is entitled morally and legally, when in the execution of his duty, to use all legitimate methods of warfare." [*] This declaration, coupled with the legalization of the IRA as Ireland's national army, gave added credence to the view of a nation engaged in war rather than an "illegal" revolution. Furthermore, these actions made legitimate the murder and boycott guerrilla tactics the rebels were forced to use, but which otherwise might have been seen by the Irish people as gratuitous acts of terrorism.

A fairly complete picture of the IRA guerrilla tactics may be deduced from two brief items written by Michael Collins. In one, a 1920 pamphlet of instructions for the IRA volunteers, Collins said: "To attack troops or police would be a mistaken policy. The method adopted should be to act in small numbers in suit-

[*] Alison W. Phillips, *The Revolution in Ireland, 1906–23,* London, 1923, pp. 117–18.

able localities, thus compelling the authorities to disperse in search of them. . . . *Destruction of communications should be carried out as systematically as possible"* (italics added). The instructions also provided detailed suggestions for carrying out this destruction. He also advised that whenever possible IRA units should fight at night in a locality familiar to all the unit's members.* And in a 1922 article for the *New York American* newspaper, Collins said: "Without her spies England was helpless. It was only by means of their accumulated and accumulating knowledge that the British machine could operate. . . . Therefore, we struck at individuals, and by so doing we cut their lines of communication and we shook their morale. . . . Only the armed forces and spies and criminal agents of the British government were attacked. Prisoners of war were treated honorably and considerately and were released after they had been disarmed." †

Because the overall objective was to make the English administration of Ireland impossible, the destruction of communications was crucial to the IRA. It was achieved directly by bombing courthouses, police barracks, post offices, coast guard stations, telephone exchanges, and lighthouses and indirectly by infiltrating IRA agents into the British intelligence service and the Post Office. This phase of the tactic was designed not merely to acquire intelligence about the British plans, but to enable the IRA to identify and mark individual members of the British Intelligence Service for execution. Collins knew that as the British were forced to replace slain intelligence officers the quality of the replacements would decline along with the quality of intelligence available to the British.

A prime example of the tactic's value is found in the IRA assassination of a man named Alan Bell. In his cover role, Bell was a colorless local magistrate; in his intelligence role, he was penetrating the relations between the Sinn Fein and various Irish banks. The importance of money to any revolutionary group is obvious, but not so the persons and procedures by which financial support is made available to them. Bell was close to

---

* *Administration of Ireland,* 1920, London, 1920, p. 60.
† MacArdle, *op. cit.,* p. 319.

success at the time the IRA identified him, ordered him dragged from a streetcar in broad daylight, and killed him in cold blood.*
Although the press denounced the assassination as a "senseless act of terrorism," like each of the intelligence service assassinations it served many purposes. First, the threat posed by Bell to the IRA was eliminated. Second, any Irish people still on the fence were made aware that the IRA was active and able to operate under the noses of the British authorities with seeming impunity. Third, the IRA volunteers gained confidence in the wisdom of Collins strategy. Fourth, members of the British Intelligence Service were at least somewhat deterred in their zeal to penetrate the IRA's operations. Fifth, the English-dominated press in Ireland, by calling such assassinations "acts of desperation," perpetuated the idea that the IRA and its insurrection should be treated lightly.

It is important to note that Collins' strategy was considered to be almost heretical by many of his critics, both in and out of the IRA. Many of the "search and destroy" advocates of an earlier generation believed that the only good Englishmen was a dead Englishmen and were in the IRA more for the satisfaction of killing Englishmen than for reasons of political freedom. There were also those who felt that the tactics suggested by Collins were somehow an admission of cowardice on the part of the IRA. These were serious objections, but Collins, by the force of his personality, was able to persevere and forge the many factions into a disciplined force willing and capable of carrying out his interdependent tactical plan.

The interaction of the communications tactic with the political and social reality of Ireland is further illustrated by the way the Dail, at Collins' urging, was able to mount an indirect attack against the entire Irish transportation system so that it couldn't be used to move British troops and military supplies. The Dail directed longshoremen not to unload cargoes known or suspected to contain military supplies and railway workers not to operate trains carrying men or materiel for the British government. In the main, this tactic was effective, but because of the financial

* *Ibid.,* p. 347.

burden of providing for workers fired for obeying the Dail orders and the possibility of an adverse reaction from the population at large, it was called off after eight months.

Another indirect attack tactic developed by Collins was designed to render the police (the Royal Irish Constabulary) impotent and thereby force the British government to call on the Army to take over the police functions of law and order. This tactic was also initiated by a Dail decree that called upon all Irishmen to boycott the RIC and its personnel. It too was effective, but required the support of IRA attacks on policemen and police stations. Also, Collins is alleged to have authorized local IRA units to shoot any young man on proof that he was about to join the RIC, and whether the allegation is true or not, in July and August 1920 only twelve native Irishmen were persuaded to join the RIC while at the same time between five and six hundred resigned from the force.*

According to the report of an RIC Division Commander quoted by Alison Phillips in *The Revolution in Ireland,* the combination of boycott and attacks produced a situation in which, on the one hand, the police were: "shut up in their barracks, watching nightly for attacks, murdered if they go out singly, ambushed if they go out in parties, liable to be shot in the back at any time by an innocent civilian, unable to get exercise or recreation except at the risk of their lives." And on the other hand, according to the RIC commander, the tactics had produced general conditions favorable for the IRA: "He [the IRA] is conducting warlike operations against us and we are not permitted to do so against him. He also enjoys the usual advantages of guerrilla warfare without suffering any of the penalties attached to it. We have to act largely on the defensive, for we have no one to take the offensive against. As far as we possibly can, we take the offensive but our blows fall on empty air, as the enemy forces at once take up the role of innocent peasants whom we must not touch." †

This phase laid the groundwork for the last—but most com-

---

* *Administration of Ireland, op. cit.,* pp. 277–78.
† Quoted in Phillips, *op. cit.,* p. 185.

plex—step of Collins tactical plan: forcing the English authorities to take punitive action against the Irish people for aiding the IRA and obstructing English civil administration of Ireland. This Collins did during the last half of 1920 by increasing the scope of IRA operations and shifting into the more conventional actions of a regular guerrilla war. Collins was successful; British were forced to evacuate the countryside, retreat to the cities, and take up fortified positions, enabling the Sinn Fein to take over the direct government of large areas of rural Ireland. The cumulative effect of these tactics was that the English authorities finally decided to undertake what proved to be a vain attempt to counter the IRA insurgency.

In December 1920 the English Parliament responded by passing a resolution that declared that a "state of insurrection" existed in Ireland, which provided the legal basis for the British authorities in Ireland to place the Crown Forces there on a wartime footing, call up reserves, and introduce the death penalty against anyone who stored arms or ammunition, took part in any insurrectionary activity, or gave asylum to members of the IRA— just the response Collins had hoped to elicit. He had never expected to defeat the British Army in a conventional war or even in a protracted guerrilla war, but rather to force the English to retaliate along lines that English public opinion would finally reject.

For example, because the boycott and terror tactics had so weakened and demoralized the RIC, the English administration attempted to revitalize the moribund force by recruiting for it in England. Those recruited, who were called the Black and Tans because of their dark green and khaki uniforms were full members of the RIC.* In addition, the RIC was bolstered by the Auxiliaries, a *corps d'élite* of rebellion breakers. The Auxiliaries, largely ex-officers of England's wartime army, should not be confused with the Black and Tans, although the two groups are nearly always lumped together. The genuine Black and Tans,

---

* It should be noted that the original Black and Tans were a famous pack of Limerick hounds, and the use of the term was also an attempt to equate the police with dogs, much as the modern American rebels call police pigs and the Vietnamese call their national police white mice.

regardless of one's opinion about the wisdom of using English-men as cops in Ireland, do not deserve their bad reputation, since it was the Auxiliaries who actually carried out the physical acts of reprisal and the executions that the Irish people have always attributed to the Black and Tans.

In any case, the Auxiliaries/Black and Tans earned the ever-lasting enmity of the Irish people, and finally, in early 1921, the English administration introduced an official policy of reprisal executions against the civilian population, signaling the begin-ning of the successful end to Collins' tactical plan. They had only to hang on until the revolt of English public opinion forced the English government to call off the reprisal executions and end the war.

The final event that illustrates the phenomenon of military failure was ending the war itself, which came abruptly on July 11, 1921, when a truce calling for a cease-fire and negotiations to settle the Sinn Fein demands for independence was agreed to between the Irish rebels and the English government. The nego-tiations came to a head on December 6, 1921; it is reported that the British Prime Minister, Lloyd George, said to the Sinn Fein delegation, led by Michael Collins: "I have to communicate with Sir James Craig tonight. Here are the alternative letters I have prepared, one enclosing the Articles of Agreement reached by H. M. Government and yourselves, the other saying that the Sinn Fein representatives refuse the Oath of Allegiance and refuse to come within the Empire. If I send [the second] letter it is war, and war within three days; which letter am I to send?" *

Collins signed the treaty and, in what proved to be a pro-phetic statement, is alleged to have said he was signing his own death warrant. The treaty, ratified by the Dail on January 7, 1922, granted dominion status with a constitution similar to Canada's for all of Ireland, but Northern Ireland was given the right to remain within the United Kingdom, which it promptly chose to do. Thus the Home Rule area that is now the Republic of Ireland

---

* Quoted in MacArdle, *op. cit.*, p. 608.

comprised only the twenty-six-county area for which the Southern Ireland parliament had previously been proposed in the Government of Ireland Act of 1920.* This treaty confirmed the fact of military failure by the English.

We should also discuss the conditions that prevailed at the time of the truce and how each side looked at its ability to resume the war if the treaty negotiations failed because it is relevant to the phenomenon of military failure.

It was estimated by General Macready at the time of the truce that he would need eighty thousand troops—an increase of 100 per cent—to "reconquer Ireland," as he put it, and that he would have to devise an absolute system of total population control.† But English public opinion was unwilling to support a massive effort to "pacify" Ireland, partly because of the strong anti-war sentiment that had emerged in England after World War I and partly because of the growing sympathy among English intellectuals for the Irish cause. There were also the practical political considerations noted by Winston Churchill and others that to tie down the great bulk of the British Army in a protracted guerrilla war would jeopardize British imperial interests elsewhere in the world. Taken together these conditions provided an overwhelming justification to end the rebellion, but,

---

* The Government of Ireland Act of 1920, as it is officially titled, called for Northern and Southern Ireland to have their own provincial parliaments, but both would continue to elect representatives to the English Parliament at Westminster. Provision was made to establish a Central Council of Ireland where delegates from the two Irish Parliaments could, if they wished, merge into a single parliament for the whole of Ireland, albeit one with no real authority. In Northern Ireland, the Ulster Unionists, largely made up of Protestants, who constituted a two-thirds majority of the total population, accepted the Act as an arrangement whereby they would continue as part of the United Kingdom and be independent of the Catholic-dominated Home Rule legislative area of Southern Ireland. However, the Act was not acceptable to the Home Rulers, who demanded that all of Ireland break completely with England, and consequently the southern parliament and the Central Council failed to materiaize. Under the Act, the Northern Ireland parliament was formally opened in June 1921 as a subordinate provincial legislature under Westminster. The Home Rulers in both the north and the south not only refused to recognize it, but deliberately set out to destroy it.

† Macready, *op. cit.* p. 562.

as we have noted, Lloyd George was apparently willing to restart the war if the Sinn Fein rejected the treaty.

There has been much speculation about whether Lloyd George seriously intended to resume full-scale war against the Irish, but it is possible that he may have been misled by the British Army, not about the methods and materiel required but about the rebels' staying power in the face of all-out war. Piaras Beaslai, in *The Life of Michael Collins*, quotes a report made by General Macready on the military situation in September 1921 to Lloyd George:

Three months ago the rebel organization throughout the country was in a precarious situation and the future from the Sinn Fein point of view may be said to have been well-nigh desperate. The Flying Columns and Active Service IRA units were being constantly defeated and broken up by the Crown forces; the internment camps were rapidly filling up, the HQ of the IRA was functioning under the greatest difficulties, many of its officers having been captured. . . . Reinforcements were pouring into Ireland. Martial law was about to be proclaimed throughout the twenty-six counties, and three months of suitable weather was still before us. . . . Such were the conditions on the 11th of July, and it is small wonder that the rebel leaders grasped at the straw that was offered and agreed to negotiations.*

These words have a familiar ring, reflecting at once the seemingly unlimited optimism, or arrogance, of conventional soldiers toward guerrilla forces as well as the implicit basis of a future, almost metaphysical, request for more men and equipment "to finish the task." (It is interesting to note that Macready later asserted that if the truce had broken down in December 1921, a hundred and fifty thousand troops would have been needed to reconquer Ireland, an increase of some seventy thousand over his pre-truce estimate to do the same job. Macready's lofty view was not shared by one of his subordinate *field* commanders, Major General Gough, who felt that the effect of reprisal warfare upon his experienced regular troops, who actually

* Beaslai, *op. cit.*, Vol. II, p. 249.

carried out the counterviolence and terror, constituted a most ignoble defeat for them because, in his words, "Law and order have given place to a bloody and brutal anarchy in which the armed agents of the Crown violate every law in aimless and vindictive and insolent savagery. England has departed further from her own standards, and further from the standards even of any nation in the world, . . . than has ever been known in history before." *

Turning to the IRA's condition at the time of the truce, it may well have been severely weakened, but this should not obscure the fact that the escalation of the war was planned by Collins to produce a military situation that would induce a *political* outcome favorable to the Republican cause, not a military victory. Collins knew that the real costs to England in resuming the war could not be reckoned in pounds sterling. Not only was the English public not willing to support a renewal of the war— neither were English troops. This underscores the final principle in a military failure revealed by Collins' tactical plan: that after the inevitable slackening of organization, discipline, and control in a status quo army during a period of truce negotiations, it is relatively difficult in terms of morale and combat efficiency, to resume hostilities if negotiations fail. In a regular soldier's mind, when a truce is announced the war is over.

It was perhaps for all these reasons that Collins incurred the wrath of a significant number of his followers who believed that because the costs of resuming the war were unacceptable to the English, he should have held out for the whole loaf. It is clear that Collins signed the treaty he believed it represented the best terms possible. He was probably also painfully aware that the British people's current mood of surrender—or, more accurately, indifference to the "Irish Question"—might turn to a mood of vengeance if the treaty terms were rejected by the Dail. It is implicit in Collins' decision that he believed the likelihood of the English opting for "total victory" over the rebels was too high for them to reject the treaty terms, and, unlike some of his

* Quoted in MacArdle, *op. cit.*, p. 448.

more headstrong followers, he knew how far the Sinn Fein and IRA had come since the Easter Rising and how difficult it would be to go any farther if the war was resumed on an all-out basis.

Although our selective survey of military failure has not been exhaustive, it does present the full spectrum of the most likely conditions and results of this phenomenon. But what does military failure really mean? We can describe it in detail. We can identify its turning point in specific instances and at a specific point in time, a point beyond which military failure becomes inevitable. We can identify and predict its path following that point. We can even determine a strategy to avoid it in the first place. But the record shows that this knowledge is not enough, because those whose ambitions, egos, and power enable them to set nations off on the path to military failure are rarely deterred by this kind of knowledge, either generally or specifically. In the military failures we have considered, the political leaders who initiated the actions were too obsessed with their immediate political problems to give much thought to the theory of the operation they were attempting, nor did their military commanders who actually carried out the operations.

In each of our examples, failure resulted from incorrect strategy in that it did not take into consideration the prevailing "objective conditions"—those circumstances beyond a nation's immediate control that have a direct bearing on the accomplishment of its objectives. Three of these conditions must be considered if failure is to be avoided: the attitudes, sympathies, and loyalties of the armed forces; the state (actual and potential) of public opinion; and the international situation—both past and present— as it impinges on the contemplated military action.

Another question political leaders must ask themselves is whether military action is appropriate in the circumstance. As our examples demonstrate, armed force is nearly always an ineffective means to force another country to accept an abstract principle such as the supremacy of a particular leader, a religious faith, or a political ideology, perhaps because so-called "moral" wars are so rarely fought for genuinely moral purposes. Obviously, military "appropriateness" is difficult to assess because political leaders tend to blur the difference between national purpose and national interest. Even so, the attempt should be made, if for no other reason than to avoid the bias in favor of using force to resolve differences that do not threaten a nation's existence.

FIVE

The Military Establishment

"This conjunction of an immense military establishment and a large arms industry is new in the American experience. . . . We recognize the imperative need for this development. Yet we must not fail to comprehend its grave implications. Our toil, resources, and livelihood are all involved; so is the very structure of our society. In the councils of government, we must guard against the acquisition of unwarranted influence, whether sought or unsought, by the military industrial complex."

—Dwight D. Eisenhower

REGARDLESS of one's views about Vietnam, the military establishment's efficiency is a matter that transcends this issue. If the military has become psychologically enfeebled and physically weakened to the point where its capacity to deter or repel real aggression is inadequate, then—in a world in which force is still very much a part of politics—our nation is in for serious trouble. The evidence indicates it has reached that point, that the fact of failure in Vietnam has already had a decidedly negative effect upon the attitudes, sympathies, and loyalties of our nation's armed forces.

This assertion is based as much on the direct evidence of widespread failures such as the *Pueblo* affair, the Green Beret murder case, the Master Sergeant's ring of shady businesses, and the My Lai massacre as it is on the indirect evidence of the qualitative and quantitative military manpower crisis. Even though official statements have blamed performance failures on a "pitiful few" and have promised to punish those responsible, an unacceptably high number of career and potential career military leaders are not convinced that the military is a profession they should pursue. For the time being, their discontent, disbelief, dissatisfaction, and indifference may remain below the surface arguments about Vietnam, but in the long run these attitudes may threaten America much more than the polarization of civilian attitudes about the Vietnam War and its aftermath. For example, let us consider the implications of three problem areas in the "military disestablishment": drugs, dissent, and race.

The traditional military attitude toward drug abuse in the military services has been to treat it as a "nonproblem"—that is, to eliminate it by confining and discharging anyone discovered to be using drugs. In each of the services, nonmedical drug use was a crime punishable by up to ten years' imprisonment, dishonorable discharge, and forfeiture of all pay and allowances. In the past, this use of punitive discharges to rid the armed forces of those drug abusers who were caught was generally successful in keeping the problem of drug abuse a relatively minor one in comparison with, for example, alcoholism and venereal disease. Consequently, military leaders and civilian officials in the Defense Department rejected any suggestion that drug abuse in the armed services had become a worldwide problem that they had to take more seriously than they had been doing since World War I. The "no-problem" myth prevailed until October 1970, when the Defense Department issued a directive authorizing—but not requiring—the services to give amnesty to anyone admitting to drug use, stating that the military departments "are encouraged to develop programs and facilities to restore and rehabilitate members who are drug users or drug addicts when such members desire." Unfortunately, the Defense Department's "encouragement" of the idea that drug addiction is a medical problem that requires special treatment and rehabilitation was and remains an idea before its time in the military services.

How the military responded to this directive is a sad commentary on the U.S. armed forces. The Marine Corps chose to ignore the amnesty program by officially saying, in effect, "Men who take drugs have no place in the Marines." The Navy, Air Force, and Army, in a hodgepodge of loosely structured programs, attempted to bring together the well-meaning but hopelessly ineffective efforts of chaplains, medical officers, and lower-level officers to lure drug abusers into treatment centers. High-level command support for these efforts was either lukewarm or nonexistent. In fairly short order the Marine Corps was forced to recant from its hard-line position when its rate of drug-abuse-per-thousand-men outstripped the rest of the services and threatened its ability to maintain its authorized active-duty strength.

For months after the directive was issued, senior military and civilian officials argued about the scope of the problem, contending that it was primarily a nuisance and an embarrassment to the field commanders and that what problem did exist was well under control. However, in a report filed April 28, 1971, by the Subcommittee on Drugs of the House Armed Services Committee, the scope of the drug problem was shown to be near epidemic proportions." "The consensus," the report said, "is that 40 to 50 per cent of the men entering military service have at least experimented with marijuana; 50 to 60 per cent . . . have at least experimented with various kinds of drugs, principally marijuana, and upwards of 10 per cent . . . could be using hard narcotics," and added that there were a hundred and sixty drug-related deaths in the military in 1970.

The report managed at least to change the thrust of the arguments about the military services' responsibility in the matter of drug abuse. They now insisted it was a "not invented here" problem, that since drug abuse exists in society as a whole and the men who come into the services are drawn from society, they bring the problem with them. Leaving aside the correctness and statistical validity of this argument, if one accepts its logic then one must also conclude that the military services are either incapable of screening out such men or are willing to let them be inducted. In any case, it does not relieve the military of responsibility for dealing with the problem. Neither does the argument that blames the escalation of the drug-abuse problem in the military services in the last three years on the de-escalation of the war. There is little disagreement that de-escalation increased the individual's inclination, and perhaps opportunity, to use drugs while in Vietnam, but for psychological reasons that transcend the Vietnam War's environment and its resulting frustrations. Therefore, because the problem of drug abuse in the military continues after the war has ended, our concern is with how the U.S. political and military leadership has responded to the broad challenge posed by the problem rather than with "the" drug problem in Vietnam. This issue also differs from the one concerning its sources and magnitude, although they are related.

Following publication of the Subcommittee's report in April 1971, and the resulting publicity, the military finally admitted that a problem existed, a problem that had been made immeasurably worse by its "search and destroy" campaign against marijuana begun in late 1968, which is generally credited with causing the swing to heroin and other hard drugs. Marijuana starred in a rerun of the World War II "VD scenario" in which, like VD, it was pictured as an evil that would damage a serviceman's brain and induce apathy that would endanger those who were dependent on him. This campaign was proclaimed a success after a week when several thousand were arrested for possession of marijuana. Good triumphed over evil, but in so doing it left the forces of good with far more serious problems than the one they thought they had solved. In the words of Dr. Norman E. Zinberg, writing in *The New York Times,* "Marijuana was for those in charge so clearly evil that they truly expected that stamping it out would be regarded as a good thing. They felt little need to wonder what had brought about this scourge; they just blamed the fact that marijuana was available."

The result of treating drug abuse as a disciplinary rather than a physiological and psychological matter and of avoiding a consideration of what responsibilities the military services have to their soldiers, sailors, airmen, and marines who had become drug abusers while on active duty, or who were potential or actual drug abusers at the time of their induction, has been to place the problem on the civilian society's doorstep. In the words of Representative John S. Monagan of Connecticut, "Thousands of addicted veterans are present in our society. In addition, there are tens of thousands of veterans who, although not drug addicts, have had their life and future impaired because of their association with drug abuse in the military. Until recently, it was not uncommon for *any* drug offense to result in a dishonorable discharge from the service. Such treatment does not help to alleviate the depression which may have led to the drug abuse in the first place." Furthermore, until the Defense Department directive authorizing amnesty for drug abusers was promulgated, the military services' policy of arrest, confinement, and dishonorable discharge deprived those so discharged of the right to eventual care in Veterans Administration facilities.

Partly because of the abortive campaign against marijuana and partly because of internal and external pressures upon the military establishment itself, the problem of drug abuse continued to grow, until by mid-June 1971 it had reached serious enough proportions that it could no longer be ignored or solved in some simplistic way. So, in what has become standard operating procedure for politicians faced with huge, complicated problems, President Nixon in a special message to Congress on June 17, 1971, declared a "war on heroin" and announced that he would seek legislation "to permit the military to retain for treatment any individual due for discharge who is a narcotics addict —all our servicemen must be accorded the right to rehabilitation."

President Nixon's statement was less a declaration of war on heroin and a commander's pledge to his troops than an exercise in political "catch-upsmanship." A month earlier Congressman Monagan had introduced legislation in the House that would prevent the discharge of addicted servicemen until judged "free of habitual dependence" by competent medical authorities. Called the Armed Forces Drug Abuse Control Act of 1971, Monagan's bill also would have established a Drug Abuse Control Corps within each branch of the armed services to offer drug education and rehabilitation and would have prohibited any person from being tried for a narcotics offense if he voluntarily agreed to undergo treatment recommended by the Drug Corps.

Monagan's bill squarely placed the drug-abuse monkey on Nixon's back by making explicit his responsibility as commander in chief to do what was necessary to "take care of his troops." Nixon evaded his responsibility by passing it along to the military services' chiefs and the Secretary of Defense, and in so doing changed the individual serviceman's "right" to rehabilitation to a command-controlled "privilege." This is no idle semantic difference; privileges can be given or taken away on the basis of agreed-to published rules or by an individual commander's personal whim or malice, while rights are those features and conditions of military life guaranteed servicemen by the Constitution and the laws enacted by the Congress.

In the legislative battle that followed the declaration of war on heroin, the administration's bill, H.R. 9503, won out over Monagan's bill. H.R. 9503 called for addicted servicemen to be kept, without their consent, for a period of thirty days beyond their scheduled discharge, during which time they would receive mandatory drug rehabilitation and education. If they required further treatment after thirty days, they would be counseled and referred to a civilian treatment program on a voluntary basis, and then discharged. No matter how serious a serviceman's addiction was, or what type, he would be treated for only thirty days, an unreasonably short time for effective rehabilitation if authorities in the drug field are to be believed about the complexities of drug treatment.

During the legislative hassle over drug abuse in the military between mid-1971 and spring 1972 no real programs were established to help addicted servicemen. While the legislators debated, the President waited, and the military establishment's leaders looked the other way, in the words of a military officer in the drug field, "tens of thousands of soldiers have gone home as walking time bombs." Several interesting facts came to light during the congressional hearings on drug abuse: out of forty-four hundred soldiers found using hard drugs between July 1 and September 10, 1971, only twenty-three volunteered for short-term treatment; throughout 1971, between one and two thousand servicemen had been discharged each month after having been twice certified as heroin users on the basis of urinalysis tests and their commanding officers' assertions that these men had made no effort to break their habit and were of "negligible value to the armed services"; and—contrary to the testimony of Pentagon officials—it was revealed that the confidentiality promised to drug abusers who volunteered for treatment was being routinely violated by the use of code numbers on their discharges indicating that they had been narcotics users while in the service. These facts, and the difficulty Congress had in getting them, tell us a great deal; for example, that the number of GI heroin addicts already discharged is unknown, but may run as high as half a million.

Since mid-1971 the statistical "decline" in drug abuse in the armed forces and the corresponding quadrupling of the death toll from heroin overdosage is explained by the fact that the stated concern of officials for those addicted was all for show and in practice was used to entrap men into admitting their afflication and then using that admission as the basis for punishing or getting rid of them, with predictable results: the troops with drug problems have no one they can turn to for help. They have been lied to, ostracized, and unfairly punished by a military system that expressed concern for them as human beings, but when the time came to translate that concern into positive, sustained action opted to cast them out rather than jeopardize the careers of those who run the system.

One can understand the military leaders' dilemma. On the one hand, as soon as the drug problem became public they had to disavow any responsibility for it because to accept that responsibility was to call into question their past performance in allowing it to occur. And, on the other, to attempt to solve the problem and fail would call into question their ability to solve future problems. As a consequence, the high command opted to get rid of the drug abusers as soon as possible, with only minimal concern for the results of this policy. In testimony before the congressional subcommittee, Dr. Judianne Densen-Gerber, executive director of Odyssey House in New York, called heroin addiction a "communicable disease" and maintained that, through a natural ripple effect, seventy-five thousand discharged service-man addicts might well produce an additional two hundred fifty to seven hundred fifty thousand addicts in the United States within a year of their return to civilian life. She warned that if servicemen are not fully rehabilitated before their release they will cause a "massive increase" in America's heroin problem.

Further, the high command's rejection of those with service-connected drug problems threatens our entire military establishment because it represents abandonment of the most fundamental principle of leadership, namely, loyalty. Without loyalty both up *and* down, no military organization can long endure let alone successfully defend a nation against its enemies. In the long run, the effects of drug abuse on those afflicted is not the most important issue for the military; rather, it is the reactions of those servicemen who are *not* drug abusers to the military system's failure to provide more than lip service to other servicemen who need real help.

In study after study of servicemen's attitudes it has been made clear that those at the tag end of the chain of command no longer believe in the integrity, honesty, and dedication of their officers, commissioned or noncommissioned, and that within the chain of command trust and confidence has largely been replaced by cynicism and wariness. These attitudes are undoubtedly the result of the military high command's abandonment of the time-proven military truth that a leader "takes care of his men—absolutely and completely." Instead, the men see a system in which those who can evade responsibility for the military's drug-abuse problem are rewarded while those who try to make good on the President and the Pentagon's pledge to those afflicted are accused of being "soft on drugs."

Further, who can calculate the effect on our servicemen of knowing that the U.S. military not only has done nothing to help addicts in the service but looks the other way when a crackdown on the production and sale of heroin might interfere with the economy of its supposed allies? What do they think, for example, of the Vietnamese children who openly sold heroin every day at a stand directly across the highway from the entrance to the headquarters of the U.S. general in command of the II Field Force at Longbinh, the largest military installation in Vietnam? Or of the fact that the vials in which heroin is sold are suspiciously uniform throughout Vietnam? Or of the "no-fire zones" designated to protect areas where opium poppies are known to be cultivated?

Turning to the problem of dissent in the armed forces, the consequences of military failure in Vietnam are more readily seen in the changed and hostile attitudes toward the military system on the part of those who are expected to run it on a day-to-day basis than they were in the case of drug use. Griping, bitching, and complaining about one's lot while in uniform is, of course, nothing new. But today's dissatisfaction with the military has taken a different turn. It is less concerned with the lack of creature comforts and directed more toward those who play by a traditional procedural book to evade their personal and professional responsibility to modify, change, or discard procedures proven to be ineffective.

There have always been a few in each branch of the military services who have questioned the old ways of doing things and risked their careers to bring about what they believed to be necessary change. They are the true innovators. In theory, the military system welcomes better ways of doing things, but like any large institution it has trouble accepting new ideas and suggestions, so it tends to have an inbuilt bias that hinders or retards the rate of change. This is not a necessarily bad thing, in that it helps to prevent change merely for change's sake, or the adoption of new procedures that may provide only marginal improvement over the old ones; but basically the military's institutional inertia tends to perpetuate vested-interest inefficiency. In the past, the military was able to handle its few dissidents by co-opting their ideas, breaking their spirit, or damning them with faint praise. For example, such evaluations as "He performed with professionalism; he is an idealist, very intelligent and well versed, but like so many who enter military service is 'typically immature' and young in respect to knowledge and adherence to the system" have been used as much to mark a young officer for increased responsibility as to warn the authorities that he may be a potential heretic.

As long as there were only a few who questioned the old ways of doing things these methods of controlling them worked reasonably well. But by late 1966 and early 1967 there began to appear, in ever-increasing numbers, a new breed of junior officers who in their education and upbringing had been taught to question everything. These junior officers, who were commissioned in the early stages of the Vietnam War, shared the views of their civilian contemporaries on race, foreign affairs, poverty, and urban problems, for example. Unlike their counterparts in the officer corps before Pearl Harbor and to a lesser degree after the Korean War, they were drawn from a broad cross section of civilian life, and as a group their academic, creative, and leadership potential was without parallel in the history of the U.S. armed forces. They accepted President Johnson's publicly stated reasons for the U.S. intervention in Vietnam—self-determination of the Vietnamese people and the necessity to stop aggression. At first these young officers provided a real shot in the arm for a military system gone stale as a consequence of Cold War tedium, and they made a significant difference in our forces' initial ability to tolerate the high level of chaos and ambiguity that is characteristic of a "peoples' war." These were the men who dutifully and effectively led the "search and destroy" missions, defoliated and bombed, and almost put the coonskin on LBJ's wall. But eventually they gave up on the war and those directing it because of their disillusionment with the system's unwillingness to examine the disparity between the actual results of the methods used to prosecute the war and its stated objectives. This was a gradual process. As their feeling of intellectual impotence about the war mounted, they became more and more frustrated; their attitude evolved into a form of passive resistance to standard military procedures, especially in the interpersonal area, demonstrated by their obvious reluctance to enforce regulations they no longer believed in and by their requests for the earliest possible release from active service.

This disaffection was largely ignored by the military hierarchy or blamed on civilian anti-war sentiment rather than on a leadership vacuum in the officer corps. By mid-1968, however, the impact was beginning to be felt in all the services. As the able junior officers left, they were replaced by less and less competent persons, of whom the epitome must be Lieutenant William Calley. In an article in the *Washington Post,* Haynes Johnson quoted a general as saying, "We shouldn't have commissioned men like Calley, but we had to. We commissioned a lot of mediocrity. And we had to. We kept people in the service that otherwise we would have discharged, because we had to meet the requirements [of the Vietnam War]."

The general's remarks underscore how the military system compounded the failure of its battlefield strategy and tactics. By accepting junior officers leadership it knew to be inferior and by not changing its strategy and tactics to account for this reality, the military hierarchy insured not only a diminished combat effectiveness, but also the creation of other problems totally beyond the ken of the system's leaders at all ranks in each of the services. Interestingly, only two solutions to the decline in the quality of U.S. military leadership have been seriously considered: an increase in pay and the provision of some "civilian comforts." The basic fallacy underlying these solutions is the assumption that traditionalist thinking among the questioning young men has been replaced by materialism and hedonism. This is not the case. The exclusive reliance on increased privileges as a substitute for motivating young men to do their best for those they lead and those they follow has only aggravated the situation.

By almost any standard of direct and indirect measurement, the conclusion is inescapable that since 1968 the quality of leadership among junior officers and NCOs in the services has consistently declined. One such measure is the drastic drop in the retention rates among those who seemed intent on military careers. For example, in 1961 about one-third of the lieutenants and captains who had entered by way of Reserve Officer Training Corps remained beyond their period of obligated service in the Army, and, in almost all cases, they stayed not only on the basis of competition but because they asked to be retained on active duty in order to become career officers. In 1972 the Army's retention rate among those eligible for such consideration was down to about 8 or 9 per cent. In 1966 the Navy retained about one out of four of the junior officers assigned to surface ships; by 1972 the rate had declined to about 15 per cent. In naval aviation the situation is even worse. In 1966 nearly two-thirds of the Navy's pilots—who are trained for about two years to qualify for carrier duty at a cost of a quarter of a million dollars each—shipped over for at least one additional tour of duty. In 1972 three out of four Navy pilots were leaving as soon as they completed their obligated service. The Navy's nuclear submarine force has fared only slightly better. Its junior officers are offered bonuses of up to $15,000 to remain in the submarine service, but their current retention rate is only 36 per cent, or just slightly more than half of what it was six years ago. And more than thirteen thousand officers who had indicated their intention of making a career in the Air Force have requested separation at the end of their present tours.

The other side of the problem is that the services are no longer able to recruit officers in sufficient number and quality to meet current requirements. For example, in 1969 the Marine Corps was approximately eight hundred short of meeting its authorized quota of three thousand new second lieutenants, in spite of the fact that that year the Marine Corps' educational requirement of a bachelor's degree or its equivalent to become a second lieutenant was reduced to two years of post-high-school education from almost any source. In the same period the Army was only slightly more successful in its search for new officers even though it completely did away with any post-high-school educational requirement—in a year in which there were nearly half a million male college graduates. Each of the services also lowered its physical requirements, to such an extent in the Army that someone who in 1964 would have been rejected on physical grounds for enlistment as a private now qualifies for appointment as a second lieutenant.

The connection between the decline in the quantity, quality, and length of service of junior officer leadership and the frequent breakdowns of the military machine is rarely made. Official military spokesmen are likely to explain the breakdowns in sociological terms—that is, for example, that the man who deserts or goes AWOL does so because of society's ills rather than because of a failure in responsible personal leadership at the small-unit level. Those who run the military system know better, but to acknowledge the cause of the breakdowns means they will have to do something about it. How long this can go on is anyone's guess, but the question may become academic because the Army may soon be unable to function in the real world. During 1969, with 1.5 million men on active duty, the Army lost ten thousand man-years of service due to men going AWOL, and well over fifty-six thousand deserted. A concrete example is the 82nd Airborne Division, stationed at Fort Bragg, North Carolina, which is supposed to be ready to deploy anywhere in the world on a few hours' notice. When the division was alerted in September 1970 to prepare to go to Jordan if necessary to protect U.S. citizens endangered by the fighting there, the division commander informed the Joint Chiefs of Staff that only one of its three brigades was able to go. At the time, the 82nd was nearly two thousand qualified men short. Since then this dangerous situation has been remedied for the 82nd, but only by robbing Peter to pay Paul; as a consequence, while today there may be one dubiously "combat ready" division in the Army it is doubtful there are two.

Massive desertion and unauthorized absence rates in turn produce badly overcrowded brigs and stockades where punishment for infractions of discipline becomes arbitrary and inconsistent and where those who are expected to lead and those who are expected to follow—after their release—become polarized into warring factions. Trust in the essential integrity of the system and those who run it is replaced by antagonism. This is the essential condition that describes today's military. And as long as overt examples of this antagonism are treated as isolated, unrelated events rather than symptoms of a leadership deficiency in the military system, it is likely to worsen.

The most extreme manifestation of the antagonism between

those who lead and those who follow is the increase of "frag-ging," described by Eugene Linden in the *Saturday Review* as "a macabre ritual of Vietnam in which American enlisted men attempt to murder their superiors." The term is derived from the fragmentation hand grenade, the weapon most often used be-cause it destroys all evidence with its explosion. Fragging is not unique to the Vietnam War; officers have been murdered by their men during every war in this century. In earlier wars, and in Vietnam until about the end of 1968, "classical" fragging generally was the result of an individual's deep personal anxiety and anger directed against a specific NCO or officer for imagined as well as real personal wrongs illegally inflicted upon him under the guise of the line of duty, or as a result of the members of a unit agree-ing to rid themselves of an inexperienced or overzealous NCO or officer who—they believed—unnecessarily and repeatedly en-dangered their lives. Since late 1968 we have seen the emergence of "modern" fragging, which differs from its predecessor. It now occurs in response to a general leadership failure and takes the form of a servicewide game of psychological warfare on the part of enlisted men against their superior officers and NCOs.

The modern fragging game involves the use of both non-lethal weapons such as hand grenades with the explosive charge removed but that still hiss and pop, to intimidate officers and NCOs, and highly destructive weapons such as booby-trapped 155-mm shells or claymore mines. The fragmentation hand gre-nade is still the most popular means, but its method of delivery has become more exotic. (It is not uncommon for officers and NCOs to make sure someone else uses the latrine before they risk sitting on a possibly booby-trapped toilet seat.)

Unlike classical fragging, modern fragging is most likely to occur in rear areas where dangers from an armed enemy are minimal, or outside of combat areas altogether, in barracks, of-fices, living quarters, and recreation centers. Nor it is limited to Southeast Asia, but occurs wherever U.S. troops are stationed, in-cluding the continental United States. The targets are also dif-ferent. In a highly classified study of the intended victims in some four hundred fifty cases of "actual and possible assault with ex-

plosive devices," no demographic or attitudinal profile domi-
nates or was even statistically significant—that is, no characteristic of background, assignment or prior performance evaluation
can account for who was fragged and who was not.

The ostensible objectives of modern fraggers are also different from those of their earlier counterparts. The testimony of
men tried and convicted for fragging in Vietnam in 1970–71 reveals that almost all the reasons they offered for the attacks were
vaguely impersonal, asocial, and lacking in a sense of passion for
or against the victim. In fact, from the trial transcripts one gains
the definite impression that the Vietnam War has produced an
Orwellian "doublespeak" reaction in the minds of many soldiers
in that words such as "murder" and "kill" have been replaced by
"neutralize" and "waste."

Obviously such a complex phenomenon as fragging cannot
be explained in terms of a mere semantic flipflop, but these men
do seem to have been successfully conditioned to accept a new
situational ethic that holds that the methods used in war to—in
Dean Rusk's words—"make the other fellow stop what he is
doing" are also highly appropriate and moral to make the sergeant or lieutenant stop what *he* is doing to the fragger and
other troops.

There are a variety of theories to explain the emergence of
modern-day fragging. Some psychiatrists believe it is the fault
of the officers themselves, some that it is the troops' way of
rejecting the self-created stresses of an authoritarian system—
meaningless "busywork" and unnecessary risks for personal gain
—and still others see it as a byproduct of a draft system that
failed to conscript a cross section of Americans for duty as common soldiers, relying almost exclusively on members of lower
socioeconomic groups to fill the war's manpower needs. These
theories and the underlying reality they at least partially reflect
begin with the Vietnam War and its inconclusive outcome as the
initiating cause of the fragging problem, but, as already mentioned, fragging is no longer confined to Vietnam, and from the
available evidence it appears that it is here to stay, at least for
the foreseeable future. How much fragging the military system

can sustain before becoming paranoid and flailing out at those who frag and those who *might* frag is a moot question. The tolerance for random nonspecific violence in a highly structured organization is low. At the very least we may assume that as an intimidating force fragging is influential enough to cause all officers and NCOs to at least consider the possibility of retaliation before giving an order to the men under them.

Dissent in the military has made a 180-degree turn from generally constructive criticism designed to change the old ways and bring about newer and better ways of doing things to a violent method whereby the dissenters are committed not to change, but to stopping the system. The resultant "institutionalization" of mutinous behavior revealed by fragging, sabotage and destruction of equipment, evasion of leadership responsibilities, and internecine conflict in the military is a tragedy of epic proportions and may be virtually impossible to stop. It threatens to set in motion repressive regressive action by the military to rid itself of dissenters, which will make constructive change even harder to achieve. It also threatens the very existence of our nation because there is no way to defend our freedoms if lawful, necessary military actions cannot be carried out.

The dual problems of race and race relations in the military, like those of drugs and dissent, can be traced to the prolonged and inconclusive nature of the Vietnam War. In recent years much has been written about the problem of race relations— that is, the interaction of the military system's institutional authority with black servicemen as members of a minority *group*. This problem differs substantially from the problem of race as a factor in the system's methods in dealing with an *individual* red, brown, yellow, or black serviceman. And because military leaders erroneously believed they had long since solved the individual problem, they ignored the group problem until it was too late to solve either one.

Throughout the racial and civil rights turbulence in the United States during the 1950s and early '60s there was an outright rejection of any suggestion that a racial problem existed in the armed forces, because they had been in the vanguard of integration since President Truman ordered the end of segregation in the military in 1948. Steps ordered by subsequent presidents to insure more equality for black servicemen were cited by civilian and military authorities to prove that integration was a reality in the armed forces, and the number of blacks reaching NCO and field-grade ranks was at an all-time high. White military leaders were smug to the point of complacency and often contended that the only feasible solution to "the" racial problem was for the civilian society to adopt the military's "schools solution." This attitude served the military system quite well. For a little more than two decades the myth was perpetuated that only a man's performance of duty mattered, not the color of his skin—"There are no white marines or black marines, only green marines" and "The only color I recognize is olive drab." But because these beliefs assumed a "no-problem" condition, they actually inhibited attempts to bring about genuine racial understanding; they helped to curb on-duty acts of blatant racial prejudice at the small-unit level but were of little consequence in terms of the overall problem. This was noted in the 1963 report to the President by the President's Committee on Equal Opportunity in the Armed Forces, which said: "There is no satisfactory method of handling complaints about racial discrimination. Conditions conducive to discriminatory practices are often not even known to commanders. The Negro serviceman may complain to his immediate superior, but it is rare that these complaints reach the attention of the base commander or members of his immediate staff. As problems become severe, they may or may not receive attention at one or more echelons in the command. In sum, there is no affirmative and continuing effort to monitor race relations problems on base." Thus, the report pointed out, some black servicemen had been forced to go outside the military system to get help, usually by writing their congressman or senator or bringing the matter to the attention of such organizations as the Urban League or the NAACP. The few black servicemen who went this route were considered to be "troublemakers" by the military power structure, and were largely dismissed as being unrepresentative. The reason so few black servicemen resorted to outside channels was also noted in the report: "There exists in the minds of many Negro personnel the fear that they will be subject to criticism and reprisal if they raise matters of this kind. Procedures must be developed which eliminate this fear and encourage them to present their complaints. Merely stating that reprisals are forbidden is not enough." In response to the publicity generated by the report, Secretary of Defense Robert S. McNamara took positive action to enforce regulations regarding nondiscrimination in on- and off-base housing, promotions, schooling, recruitment, and assignments, with good results. By the time the United States actively entered the Vietnam War with ground troops in March 1965 the morale of individual black servicemen was at an all-time high.

At first there was no outward indication of the nature, intensity, and scope of the racial problems building in each of the services. Military commanders were quick to point out that black fighting men had proven themselves in combat—winning, in fact, more than one-fifth of the Medals of Honor awarded. The contention was true, but those who used it as a measure of the black serviceman's tacit affirmation that institutional racism had been eliminated in the military were sadly mistaken, just as they were about the necessity for black servicemen to "prove" something in combat. Blacks had proved their courage as combat soldiers and leaders of combat forces in every U.S. war, including the American Revolution—a fact that was not mentioned by the armed forces' Information and Education Programs until racial disturbances erupted in the military services. This historical oversight may be partially explained, but not condoned, by the fact that until the Vietnam and Korean wars blacks were not included in combat ranks until the manpower crunch became severe. More typically, up to that point they were limited to serving as cooks, bakers, and labor troops. But when the first American combat units landed in Vietnam, almost a quarter of the troops were black. They were professionals, and they were there from the start.

But from about the time of the murder of Martin Luther

King the mood of black enlisted men coming into the services changed. Increasingly, black GIs in Vietnam and those about to be sent there echoed the rhetoric of Malcolm X, Stokely Carmichael, Eldridge Cleaver, and H. Rap Brown, asking, "Why should I defend someone else's freedom if no one defends mine?" This question was not answered by the military power structure, partly because it was not concerned with such abstract notions as freedom, liberty, and justice and partly because combat duty in Vietnam tended to make this issue seem unimportant. However, the temporary alliances between blacks and whites fostered by the pressures and strains of combat disintegrated almost completely when the troops left Vietnam.

Since 1967 seventy-five thousand black GIs and Marines have returned each year from combat tours in Vietnam convinced that "whitey" is not only hypocritical about matters of racial discrimination but not very bright about how to fight a war. These men, completing their military service at stateside bases, have forcefully confronted the military power structure with the necessity of coping with the problems of race and race relations in the armed services. In a prophetic statement of what lay ahead, Colonel Louis S. Hollier, U.S. Marine Corps, head of the Ad Hoc Committee on Equal Treatment and Opportunity at Camp Lejeune, North Carolina, reported to the Commanding General of the Second Marine Division on April 22, 1969:

Despite policies emanating from the highest echelons of Government down to and including those of the commanding general, and as further expressed by organizational commanders within the division, a racial problem of considerable magnitude continues to exist and, in fact, may be expected to increase.

There are two major aspects to this problem. First, is that this division and the Marine Corps are returning marines, both black and white, to civilian society with more deeply seated prejudices than were individually possessed upon entrance to service. These marines are potentially susceptible to the militant doctrines and policies of racial extremists. Second is that conditions exist within the division which could readily cause a minor incident not necessarily containing racial overtones to expand to a major racial confrontation.

Sadly, Colonel Hollier's prediction and advice to do something about the problem before it was too late went unheeded. When the commanding general to whom the report was directed was transferred, the new general who took charge was reassured by members of his staff that "old Lou is exaggerating and has become a little soft on the issue." Later events proved Colonel Hollier was only premature. On the night of July 20, after an enlisted men's dance, a group of thirty black and Puerto Rican marines attacked fourteen whites. A week later Corporal Edward E. Bankston, a thrice-wounded Vietnam veteran, died as a result of massive head injuries sustained in an unprovoked assault related to the earlier attack. In a series of subsequent racial clashes, fifteen Caucasian marines were injured by a marauding group of thirty to fifty blacks of the 2nd Marine Division. Undeclared race war appeared to be breaking out at Camp Lejeune. Between January and August 1969 more than one hundred sixty assaults, muggings, and robberies occurred on base.

The events at Camp Lejeune were typical of what was going on in the other services at U.S. bases in the United States and overseas. Reports of shootings, mutinies, and weapons thefts became commonplace. Clearly, something had to be done. The first top-ranking official to admit publicly that black-white friction was a real problem that required immediate and effective action was Marine Corps Commandant General Leonard F. Chapman, Jr., who in a September 1969 message to all marines, said: "During the past several months there have been instances among marines of violence and other unacceptable actions which apparently stem from racial differences. Such problems are almost unheard of among marines in combat. It is when marines move to other areas or return to the United States that these differences arise, and it is there where acts of violence between marines are occurring—acts which cannot be tolerated and must stop."

There is no doubt that General Chapman's acknowledgment of a serious racial problem in the Marines made top-level civilian and military authorities more conscious of the situation, and Chapman deserves recognition for his courage. But however sincere he may have been—and anything that threatens the Marines' fighting *ésprit de corps* is a no-nonsense matter for the commandant—his objective was easier said than accomplished. High-ranking officers have been too long insulated from the reality of the day room, the enlisted men's "club," and the PX to comprehend all the factors that affect the attitudes of black enlisted men. Following Chapman's call to arms, "the" race problem in the military became a matter of high-level public concern. The resulting fuss and feathers—the formation of committees, study groups, race relations councils—was typical. And it was all based on the untested assumption that racial differences could be attributed to a "lack of effective communication at the junior levels of command, as well as vertically between the young marine and his commander."

How far the situation had really deteriorated was revealed by a black staff sergeant quoted in *Armed Forces Management* magazine: "Words is all we ever get. Man, what we want is real action out of that Pentagon. We want something to happen to rid the country of discrimination against the blacks. We want the military to lead the way. I guess we gotta burn the place down before somebody realizes they better listen."

The anguish and frustration underlying these words tell us of a problem of gross proportions that is obviously beyond the military's capacity to solve if it relies on public statements and study groups. The plain fact is that not one of the various programs started by the military in the past four years to deal with the problems of race and racial discrimination has helped to alleviate the situation. If these programs are judged in terms of their ability to change the basic perceptions of black servicemen of whites and vice versa, they must be seen as an abysmal failure. If their purpose was to hasten complete and utter polarization of the races within the services, however, they have been a resounding success. This antinomical result can be explained by the conditions surrounding our military failure in Vietnam, and, one might suggest, was a predictable consequence of that failure.

To explain. Between March 1965 and September 1969 the

nature of race and racial discrimination problems in the services changed, partly because of the connection black servicemen made between their rights in the military and the broader question of civil rights in American society, and, more importantly, because of the black man's growing awareness of his individual worth. The phrase "I am a man" said it all, but it was misinterpreted as a threat to the system. So, because they couldn't understand what they heard, the military leadership wasted precious time seeking an answer to the question, "What does the black serviceman want?" The question was answered not only by the statement "I am a man" but unambiguously by L. Arnold Bennett, the top-ranking black in the Defense Department (Deputy Assistant Secretary of Defense for Civil Rights), who patiently told his uncomprehending superiors in 1970: "He [the black serviceman] wants the same things a white serviceman wants: respect for his personality as a man; fairness in selection for duty details; fairness in selection for educational and training opportunities; fairness in assignments to positions of supervision, high trust and responsibility; fairness in promotion; and an appreciation of and recognition for meritorious performance."

Even in peacetime the military would find it difficult to accept and act on such wise counsel, because equity in these matters is as much conjectural as it is objective, but the war made things worse. War by its very nature is unfair to those who must wage it, and in a combat situation it is all but impossible to ease the differences between those who command and those who carry out orders and simultaneously for those in command to deal with racial antagonisms. And the Vietnam War in particular made it more difficult still, because of paradoxes revealed as a result of the military failure taking place. One paradox was that of trying to bring about the kind of equity Bennett was talking about not only within an autocratic organization such as the military, but within one that was itself being actively used to perpetuate inequity and injustice in Vietnam.

The challenge of making the military system's commitment to egalitarianism believable to those at the bottom of the pyramid is overwhelming. The experience of black servicemen in Vietnam suggests that they have partially resolved the equity paradox to their advantage by manipulating their manipulators in such a way that the manipulators develop a reverse identification with those they think they are manipulating. Put another way, the officers and NCOs sent by the system's hierarchy to make the commitment to egalitarianism believable (without any accompanying structural changes in the system) to those denied it can be made to identify with them so that they, too, join the ranks of the discriminated. Likewise, the military system's hierarchy can also be made to identify with their subordinates to the extent that their verbal commitment to egalitarianism can be used to force a structural change in the military system itself. By compelling the manipulator and the system's hierarchy to accept their point of view, those who are supposed to be manipulated can resolve the equity paradox by psychological means as well as by drastic means such as the threat of an anonymously delivered hand grenade.

Theoretically it is feasible to do the same thing in a noncombat environment, but it is much more difficult because of newly created stereotypic myths about the black serviceman and his inner motivations. The black servicemen who demand their rights (one does not *ask* for one's rights) have created anxieties in the military system's white power structure and in the white majority in the system itself. Since this behavior is considered to be "different" from earlier behavior (based on earlier stereotypes), it has produced a schizophrenic, almost paranoid response in the military system. The white power structure sees the black servicemen's activism not only as a personal threat but as a threat to the system's "good order and discipline."

Navy Chaplain Richard A. McGonigal, who helped to develop the training techniques for CAP (Combined Action Platoon) Marines in Vietnam and who is co-director of the Navy's Human Response program, predicts that these perceptions may result in increased institutional racism, more disagreement about basic values between races, less accurate communication, fewer human resources, and less control of those resources. His assessment is based on a thorough study of the conditions resulting from our military failure in Vietnam, and his prediction will probably come true unless there is a major restructuring of the military system in the very near future.

McGonigal's study reveals a war that is being fought every night wherever servicemen gather. Incident after incident drives home a grim message to the military leadership about what that war is doing to our armed forces' ability to defend our nation, but this message is consistently ignored or misunderstood. Consider one incident, which took place in Koza, Okinawa. (It might just as easily happen tonight in Frankfurt, Danang, San Diego, or Cicero.) A white soldier asks a black woman marine for a dance in a bar near "Four Corners." The woman's black escort objects. Someone asks what a white soldier is doing in a "brothers'" bar anyway. A fight starts. Knives appear. The white soldier is hospitalized. The black soldier is confined to the brig and assigned legal counsel. The bar is placed off limits by the provost marshal. The Okiniwan witnesses ask each other about American democracy. When the other men get back to the barracks, rumors start to fly. Tomorrow night extra MPs will be needed just to maintain the poor level of control of tonight.

In incidents such as this McGonigal sees a fourfold problem that, because of the way the military system's white power structure responds to it, poses a distinct threat to the ability of the armed forces to carry out their assigned missions. First, in his example, institutional racism is seen in the segregated bar, the immediate confinement of the black soldier, the necessity to provide legal counsel for the defendant, and the fact that it is the blacks' bar which is placed off limits. Second, disagreement about basic values has much to do with why these servicemen informally segregated their bars and why the white soldier misjudged the advisability of asking the black woman marine to dance. Third, inaccurate communication is an almost inevitable result of white authority figures moving into a bar for blacks to see that "justice" is done. Fourth, two soldiers were no longer available for duty and neither is made more excited about reenlisting. And so it goes . . . increased institutional racism; more disagreement about values; less accurate communication; and reduced supply and control of personnel.

Neither the legal correctness of the military system's response to this incident nor the fact that the tactics used were similar to those used in the past to keep racial peace is the issue. What is important is that most black servicemen consider this kind of response to be "pacification by resegregation," and thus it is ineffective. To a degree not yet measurable, these changes in the attitudes of the black serviceman toward the power structure are becoming irreversible. McGonigal notes that, since late 1969, in the wake of expressions of high-level concern about the problems of race and racial discrimination in the military there has been a growing disparity between the values of whites and blacks in each of the services' enlisted ranks. This disparity is significant because clusters of values become ideologies that can and do steer, canalize, and actually define the needs of those who hold them. He cites recent studies made by Navy Commander Robert Beddingfield at three Marine Corps bases that indicate the value clusters of black marines are centering more upon dignity, pride, and the importance of individual liberty while those of white marines are moving toward security, health, and material wealth, and that the two groups appear to be closing and becoming less tolerant of each other.

There are some negative characteristics of how the military operates that affect the areas we have just discussed as well as all aspects of the system. They are not new, but because of the problems that have been made more severe by the military failure in Vietnam, we are able to see them more clearly and to be more aware that they make it exceedingly difficult for the military to come to grips with its problems.

One of these characteristics is the "passive-aggressive" response of those who command to those who are expected to carry out the orders. In each of the problem areas we have examined, the military hierarchy initially either consciously ignored or minimized the fact that the men themselves were virtually disregarding their leaders' authority and responsibility. By its inaction in the face of recalcitrant behavior, the system's leadership tacitly condones opposition to its efforts and appears to be passive concerning the necessity either to carry out orders or to change them if they are irrelevant. This passivity in turn inevitably leads to an aggressive response on the part of those at even higher levels of authority in the system, because the almost institutionalized insubordination inherent in an undisciplined situation breeds its own form of violence and threatens the system's very structure. Thus, in an Orwellian sense, leadership failure creates a condition in which "passive is aggressive."

This doesn't mean the military should return to a simpler time when orders were obeyed just because they were orders, but rather it should help us understand why it is necessary for military leaders to engage in self-examination and self-criticism, to change what needs to be changed, and to explain those changes in such a way that those who carry out the orders understand and support them. This is what "good order" (efficient performance) and discipline are really all about, and neither is achieved if those in charge attempt to command before they lead.

Command, in the broadest meaning of arbitrariness, pettiness, insensitivity, and isolation from its ostensible objects, has characterized the performance of the military system's leadership in the past several years. To rid the military of the petty and not-so-petty tyrants who believe that discipline means keeping men busy at meaningless tasks and unimaginative training or enforcing punitive regulations for regulations' sake alone requires more and better control over everyone in the chain of command. The situation has become so bad that only by such additional control can the means be found to provide increased *internal* controls in individuals, the *sine qua non* of modern military discipline, which relies on persuasion, manipulation, and group consensus to maintain each unit's integrity. But to increase the amount of control over those at the base of the pyramid—even for the most noble objectives—is to run the risk of evoking a violent response from the anti-authoritarian groups in the military, with the subsequent use of an inordinate amount of force to put down such a response or to enforce the control measure itself. As with fragging, the potential for a mutinous refusal to carry out an order is so widespread that routine actions are being avoided by those in charge. The result is that the federal government is less and less able to extend its will through its military forces, whether in riot control, mutual security assistance, or constabulary activity overseas.

The real tragedy of these problems is that we avoid connecting the events which, taken together, indicate a disturbing degree of erosion of moral principle within the military. We rationalize the failures. We forget quickly, almost as if by forgetting we can prevent a repetition of the failures. Maybe there are reasons other than a lack of leadership for My Lai, the heroine epidemic, racial violence, the bogus award of the Silver Star to a general in Vietnam, the conviction of the Provost Marshal General—the top cop of the Army—for his illegal extracurricular activities, the PX scandals, widespread cost overruns, and financial mismanagement. Maybe the modern military manager-bureaucrat has to be too many things to too many masters to know what his men are actually doing in the field, the barracks, on liberty, and in their dealings with the civilian side of the military-industrial-university complex. Maybe Vietnam was such a different kind of war that it could be fought successfully with scarcely any immediate supervision of officers above the rank of lieutenant. Personally, I doubt it.

There is considerable evidence to suggest that the lack of supervision is deliberate, the result of a perception of how one satisfies one's superiors and gets ahead in the military system. Lucian K. Truscott 3d, the son of a World War II general who is himself a retired Army colonel who commanded infantry units in Korea and South Vietnam, noted, in *The New York Times:* "A West Point classmate and friend of mine, recently promoted to brigadier general, admitted to me that he found he had to be dishonest to 'do well' as a battalion commander in Vietnam. He had to falsify reports simply because there were not enough hours in the day to get everything done or undone. He had to lie to pass inspections and training tests; to control AWOL rates and court-martial rates and venereal disease rates; to keep ahead of his peers on all of the numbered charts that today measure success. Besides, he reports, 'Everyone else was doing it.' He had to be corrupt, for if he had not been, would he have been promoted to colonel, and then to brigadier general—and on and on?" Colonel Truscott is describing the bureaucratic instinct for self-preservation mixed with individual lust for advancement-no-matter-what, careerism corrupted by careerists who know their performance will be evaluated by their peers on the basis of their reports.

One consequence of our failure in Vietnam has been to reveal and accelerate this corruption, but its existence antedates our combat involvement in Vietnam and must be understood in context if it is to be eradicated. It is the product of a selection/promotion process that is an exercise in image-making rather than a means of honestly evaluating the basic competence of the officer corps. Since the end of the Korean War the art of being promoted has been refined into a science by those seeking high rank. Few civilians realize that in wartime military public relations men spend a great deal of time making people believe in the imagery of generals and admirals, doing a rerun of "Horatio Alger Dons Khaki" on behalf of their clients. Another aspect of the "Selling of the Pentagon" is the attempt to promote top-level military leaders as infallible authorities on military matters. In this context, one of the greatest "military" disappointments of the Vietnam adventure has been that it revealed high-level incompetence for all to see, despite all efforts to hide it behind a screen of self-protecting secrecy.

A look at the military's "promotion game" will show that it was not only a contributing cause to military failure in Vietnam but that it stands in the way of dealing constructively with the unhealthy consequences of that failure as they affect the military establishment. The promotion game has been changed from the way it was played in pre-World War I days. According to General Maxwell D. Taylor, in *Swords and Plowshares,* when he joined the Army in 1922 "promotion was strictly by seniority, and a large bloc of temporary officers taken into the Regular Army at the end of the war [World War I] constituted a discouraging 'hump' in the promotion list just ahead of my contemporaries and me. As a result it took me thirteen years to become a captain, and such distinguished officers as Generals Gruenther, McAuliffe,

Palmer, and Wedemeyer, who graduated a few years before me, took seventeen years. Under such conditions of stagnation, many of the most promising young officers resigned and sought their fortune in civil life. But for some unaccountable reason a remarkable number stayed in the service to become the military leaders of World War II. *In these doldrums, they were saved by some inner feeling of the importance of their profession* [italics added]." But in the post WW II era in the attempts to prevent a return to the "conditions of stagnation" that prevailed between the world wars a crudely competitive system for promotion was created that tended to bolster young officers' motives to "win" the game instead of strengthening their "inner feeling of the importance of their profession." In short, service in the officer corps became less of a *profession* and more of a job in which the job holders and seekers chased after irrelevant results and, consequently, were not prepared for the grave responsibilities of command, high or low.

The standards of performance for an officer of the armed services have not changed much since the days of the Roman legions: success in combat, devotion to duty, professional and technical competence, leadership ability, tenacity, honor, aggressiveness, and so on. It is the process of evaluating these factors that has been corrupted; today the military establishment is caught in a measurement syndrome that substitutes numbers for personal observation. As a former member of the military I know well its peculiar obsession with getting numbered results, be they a unit's contribution to the United Givers Fund or its claimed body count. I also know that this attitude virtually guarantees a poor harvest of leaders and is wasteful and destructive.

Under the old rules, promotion was strictly based on a combination of seniority and excellence of performance. Under the new rules there is a rigid measurement scale on which to judge all leadership qualities, including such abstract but basically moral considerations as "devotion to duty." Thus the evaluation of an officer's devotion to duty—and all the other qualities as well—has become so institutionalized that it can be figured to within four decimal points, and because the number of high-ranking officers is finite and ties must be broken in deciding promotions, just one slip on a man's "devotion to duty" scale can eliminate forever his chances of making general or admiral.

It's easy to picture the results of this kind of mechanistic process: an officer willing to sacrifice the emotional (and sometimes physical) well-being of his troops and willing to follow orders he knows to be wasteful and counterproductive if not doing so might affect his superiors' evaluation of his "single-minded" devotion to duty. That this kind of unthinking, insensitive behavior in turn results in losing the confidence and support of the men an officer's "devotion to duty" is supposed to protect and defend is one of the tragic results of the current version of the military promotion game.

This procedure has been described as a dog show in which an officer's actual positive performance has less to do with how he is evaluated than his performance image, which tends to reflect the in-breeding produced by the self-perpetuating method of general-admiral selection and promotion. There is no room for innovators, mavericks, or those with unique talents in such a procedure. Those who avoid responsibility and the difficulties of real leadership inevitably look best in the judging ring, for—in this system—those who don't make waves won't fail; they will present a clean, unambiguous picture in terms of standardized "fitness" and "efficiency" reports. This mindless adherence to the letter but not the spirit of leadership has elevated the standards of middle-class don't-rock-the-boat morality to a canon of faith in the selection of those who will have life-and-death powers over the men who serve under them, and who will be making top-level military judgments for the United States for years to come.

As we have already suggested, the current critical condition of the military is primarily due to America's failure in Vietnam. Perhaps if the war had been either decisively won or lost the internal deterioration would have been arrested. What the war did was to fully and finally reveal the military's inconsistencies and contradictions to those who actually have to make it work. In the past, members of this group were motivated to try to overcome their doubts about military efficacy because of its uninterrupted record of success. But no more. The young professional military leader's disenchantment with the system stems not solely from the broad moral-political issues of Vietnam, but more from his recognition that it is almost totally unresponsive to internal pressures for change and reform. As Colonel Truscott has noted, none of the many scandals involving senior officers was brought to light by the Army. An unwillingness to clean one's own house makes a mockery of words such as duty, honor, and country, and from this realization has come the young professional's rejection of a military career.

For far too long the United States was able to pursue the failure in Vietnam because high-ranking military leaders could not or would not acknowledge freely the disasters that followed every official pronouncement about the war. They continued to support a war in which human beings by the tens of thousands were slaughtered for no real military advantage, a war that could not, because of political preconceptions and misconceptions, achieve the objective of "winning the hearts and minds" of the Vietnamese people. Furthermore, what can we reasonably expect from a military establishment when those who might expect to become generals or admirals under an honest selection process conclude that trading their integrity and right to disagree for the dubious privilege of high rank is a bad bargain? The answer is, not much. One young major, a West Point graduate, summed up the reactions of many when upon his return from overseas he asked his father, a four-star general, "But why didn't any of you who were supposed to be running the war speak up about what was wrong?" The general had no reply.

All the problems discussed in this chapter could be solved if only they were faced honestly and openly. But no one who has observed the mood of the country as it seems to be turning inward and to the right can be optimistic about the prospects for a genuine, unemotional, objective, structural reform of the military. However, without such a reform the United States will be confronted with even greater problems. The decline in military efficiency occasioned by the loss of young officers able and willing to lead involves more than just numbers. U.S. global strategy is based on an increased dependence on sophisticated military hardware, which makes the military leader's role far more complicated than in the past. He must be much more highly trained in the technical aspects of modern warfare, and as those who possess critical skills leave military service, who will be left to make intelligent, comprehensive decisions about, for example, "to ABM or not to ABM" or whether to come to the assistance of Israel?

Because force is still very much a part of world politics, we may conclude that one consequence of U.S. military failure in Vietnam is the increased probability of political-military adventurism in other parts of the world, not because the United States would not intervene with military forces, but precisely because our intervention would not be effective. This may be the ultimate irony of America's military failure in Vietnam: the same lack of high-quality leaders who should have been able to keep us out of Vietnam may, in the future, get us into an equally futile situation somewhere else.

SIX

The Cautious Government

"If thought corrupts language, language can corrupt thought. Political language is designed to make lies sound truthful and murder respectable, and to give an appearance of solidity to pure wind. One cannot change all this in a moment, but one can at least change one's own habits. . . ."

—George Orwell

ALTHOUGH there may be some validity, on some occasions in history, to the notion that a country cannot afford to fight a war and carry out domestic reform simultaneously, this "guns or butter" explanation is inadequate to account for the U.S. government's poor performance on the home front during the Vietnam War. What seems to be more important is the power of the belief, in both Washington and the nation at large, that a government that could not conclude the war in Vietnam successfully cannot cope with domestic problems any more effectively. There is a certain psychological logic in this seeming non sequitur; failure is seldom a localized disease in the body politic.

It is safe to assume that the change from activism to caution in the government's approach to domestic problems was caused in large part by growing public dissatisfaction with the war's progress and an ever-clearer awareness of its probable outcome. This questioning of governmental ability set in motion a process of public consciousness-raising wherein the same sort of questions were asked about our failure in other "wars"—those on crime, poverty, illiteracy, disease, environmental deterioration, and so on. Inadequate answers to these questions caused increasingly vocal frustration and raised an ultimate question, particularly among the young, that struck fear in the hearts of politicians and bureaucrats alike: "What is the purpose of government?"

The question is not nearly so abstract as it might seem. It refers, in this case, to the fact that for the government to pursue its various wars—domestic or otherwise—the middle class must at least remain politically neutral about these issues. Before the facts and the costs of our military failure in Vietnam were revealed to—and believed by—the general public, the federal government was able to do pretty much whatever it chose to do. But in early 1968, after it was made clear that the United States had reached a military impasse in Southeast Asia and amid further revelations of additional failures in the domestic wars, the middle class made it quite clear that the primary concern of those who ran the national government had better be the protection of property rights and not the "self-determination" or "liberation" of the downtrodden. The status quo forces at both parties' presidential nominating conventions called upon the government to give up or curtail efforts aimed at structural reform and to concentrate on enhancing the government's functional capabilities.

The first half of the message was received loud and clear by most members of Congress who were up for re-election and by most members of the career bureaucracy. It was a message they were willing to heed, because no political authority welcomes structural changes originating outside its immediate span of control and because no one feels it necessary to insist on effective action on behalf of the poor and the minorities, since they do not constitute a real power bloc. Official attention was thus focused on the politically perceived need to provide security to those who felt menaced by their fellow men—both at home and abroad.

"Security" has turned out to be a broad concept, ranging from what must be done to increase "law and order" to how to bail out near-bankrupt corporations and how to minimize the potentially damaging effects of competition in ideas, things, and between peoples. Success in achieving this kind of security has proven to be elusive; all the government's efforts to protect the middle class from the real and imagined vicissitudes of "competition" have been costly and ineffective, and in most cases have either created new problems and fears or added to existing ones.

Witness the emergence of what has been called the threat of a "dossier dictatorship." Professor Arthur R. Miller of the University of Michigan Law School describes it this way: "Americans are scrutinized, measured, watched, counted, and interrogated by more government agencies, law enforcement officials, social scientists, and poll takers than at any time in our history, and the information-gathering and surveillance activities of the federal government have expanded to such an extent that they are becoming a threat to several basic rights of every American—privacy, speech, assembly, association, and petition of government."

Professor Miller's contentions were almost immediately disputed by Assistant Attorney General William H. Rehnquist (now a Supreme Court justice), who told a Senate subcommittee investigating the executive branch's political-surveillance operations that "self-discipline on the part of the executive branch will provide an answer to virtually all of the legitimate complaints against excesses of information gathering." But as Senator Sam J. Ervin, Jr., chairman of the Subcommittee on Constitutional Rights, was to find out after Rehnquist testified, the executive branch's "self-discipline" was neither sufficient to prevent the Army from gathering information on the political affairs of a host of national, state, and local officials, political contributors, newspaper reporters, lawyers, and church figures, as well as activist radicals, nor to offer hard evidence that the practice had, in fact, been stopped. All that Ervin found out was that the operation had been transferred from the Army to the Internal Security Division of the Justice Department. Questions such as who actually ordered the political surveillance in the first place, who ordered it to be continued during the Nixon administration, and what use was made of the information gathered were never answered. So much for self-discipline's ability to answer legitimate complaints.

The political surveillance carried out by the Army under the executive branch's order differs from the largely automatic legal acquisition of data the government seeks or acquires when a citizen files a tax return, seeks government benefits, applies for a government job, or is arrested. It was designed to gain information about individuals without their consent or knowledge, and because there was no proximate evidence to indicate that those placed under surveillance had been or were involved in any criminal act, it was completely illegal. The FBI, under the leadership of J. Edgar Hoover and William Sullivan, the head of the Bureau's Domestic Intelligence Division, would have no part of this surveillance, hence the decision to make use of the Army. The ostensible rationalization for allowing the Army to carry out such a program was to "maintain information about people and forces which constitute a danger to public order." However, one of the domestic spies for the Army was closer to the truth when he said, "The Army wanted to determine their political views so that in certain situations we would know how they would react."

In fairness to the Nixon administration, it must be noted that in 1971, when the Army's excesses in the field of internal security first came to its attention, the President took prompt and decisive action to stop the program. Then, as we have noted, it was transferred to the Justice Department, where it has since been deescalated to a standby planning operation designed to operate within the scope of presidentially approved and specifically directed internal-security procedures. However, in spite of Nixon's orders, there is no proof positive that his orders have been completely complied with by those who actually run the Army's intelligence operation, since they enjoy a power and continuity that is effectively greater than that of elected and appointed officials.

We should also note that President Nixon, in spite of his apparent difficulties in extending the presidential writ over America's military intelligence bureaucratic fiefdoms, has reduced by 90 per cent the number of authorized wiretaps in connection with *all* internal and national security matters annually authorized during the Kennedy-Johnson era. This fact doesn't square with popular opinion, but it is correct; the inability of the Nixon administration to convince the public is a measure of the general paranoia induced by events of the past. In one sense the American people are perversely comfortable with their paranoia and would perhaps reject evidence that a single private investigation firm is currently operating ten times as many wiretaps in the nation's capital as the FBI operates in the entire nation.

If the future of our activities in Vietnam had not been so uncertain, it is unlikely that government officials would have felt political surveillance of law-abiding citizens was a necessary or justifiable means to preserve internal security. Nonetheless, this activity tended to increase a fatalistic feeling on the part of an American public that had become inured to accept an organized massive violation of their fellow citizens' civil liberties as a nominal and necessary action of government. According to a 1971 CBS public-opinion survey, more than 60 per cent of adult Americans considered the protection afforded them by the Bill of Rights to be irrelevant on the rather curious grounds that those who obeyed the laws didn't need the protection and those who disobeyed them shouldn't have it.

Another consequence of our military failure in Vietnam is seen in the government's efforts to placate the bureaucracy (both military and civilian) and in the shouldering aside of truly competent professional bureaucrats by public-service dilettantes, beginning with executive and legislative acceptance of the idea of wage comparability between persons in business and government as the proper criteria on which to determine government pay.* How much this idea has cost is revealed by the fact that

---

* Taylor Branch, in "The Rising Profits of Public Service" (*Washington Monthly,* March 1971), wrote: "On January 8, 1971, when he signed the Federal Pay Comparability Act of 1970, President Nixon assumed almost exclusive control over salary policy. Two of his employees, the Director of the Office of Management and Budget (OMB) and the Chairman of the Civil Service Commission, take the figures from a survey of salaries in private industry and make obscure but controversial adjustments to produce a new pay schedule which will keep federal pay comparable with private enterprise. Their recommendation becomes effective automatically each year without congressional involvement, except in the unlikely event that the President should disagree with them and propose an alternative. This cen-

since passage of the Salary Reform Act of 1962 just prior to the Cuban Missile Crisis, the total U.S. government civilian payroll has gone from $25 billion to approximately $65 billion. In this same regard, more grotesque is the fact that the fiscal 1974 defense budget shows an increase of $5.4 billion over fiscal 1973, from $76.4 billion to $81.8 billion. This increase, the budget message states, is "primarily as the result of an additional $4.1 billion required to maintain military and civilian pay levels comparable to those in the private sector, to raise pay and benefit levels sufficient to achieve an all-volunteer force, to meet normal price increases, and to pay for higher military retirement annuities."

Joseph Califano, President Johnson's special assistant for domestic affairs, writing in the *Washington Post,* noted the following facts: the proportion of the defense budget devoted to manpower costs for an all-volunteer force in fiscal 1974 will be 56 per cent, whereas in fiscal 1968 the proportion of the combined draft and volunteer force was 42 per cent; in 1968 manpower costs were $32.6 billion, but in 1974 they will be $43.9 billion, an increase of $12.3 billion; in 1968 the end strength of the armed forces was 3,547,000 men and women, while in 1974 it will be 2,233,000, a reduction of 1,314,000. Thus, Califano concludes, an all volunteer force 37 per cent smaller than a combined volunteer and draft force will cost over 30 per cent more.

Whether wage comparability will get us the *kind* of all-volunteer force and civilian bureaucracy we want is an unresolved question. Lest the reader construe this to be an argument for underpaying the military and civilian bureaucracy to keep them "poor but honest," it should be noted that wage comparability means that the government accepts the wages and salaries paid to employees in the private sector as fair noninflationary compensation, no more and no less. As such, comparability is no more likely than underpaying to insure good performance on the part of government employees; however, it frequently results in inferior performance on the part of those

tralization of control, along with the prospect of *perpetual pay increases* [italics added], is the culmination of continuing changes in the pay structure which began with the Salary Reform Act of 1962."

who are capable of much better effort because it largely takes away the incentive of pay tied to performance.

A look at the widespread phenomenon of massive cost overruns in the Pentagon's procurement of war materials will help us understand how the professional bureaucracy was quieted, bypassed, and then left to inherit the difficulties occasioned by the public-service dilettantes' attempts to make the world over. I don't mean to imply that overruns never occurred in pre-Kennedy-administration days, but it is a fact that only one of the major weapon systems conceived by Kennedy's "new bureaucracy" was brought in on-the-money and on time—the Polaris system. It may be argued, however, that this one success was made possible because the New Bureaucracy was not involved in the Polaris project and because Admiral Hyman Rickover was able to motivate and lead the men working on it.

Many explanations have been offered for the problems of cost overruns, ranging from collusion between a particular armed service and a contractor to galloping inflation and rapid technological advances that increase the complexity and the cost of weapon systems. Although these reasons are partially correct, they are really only symptoms of a larger cause: the unchecked arrogance of the civilian-turned-bureaucrat who ignored the hard-won wisdom of those whose profession encompassed the "art of the possible."

Much of the trouble originated with the Total Package Procurement (TPP) contract inaugurated in early 1961 by Secretary of Defense Robert McNamara, ostensibly to eliminate Pentagon waste. A TPP contract called for a basic price that covered development, testing, and production runs and which, if the Pentagon exercised successive options, could run for years. On the surface, the concept seemed to be a positive innovation, since it was designed to lock the producer into a long-term fixed-price contract. However, it was based on flawed premises. First, it was assumed the producer would absorb unforeseen cost increases incurred during the development and testing on the unproven theory that he would accept initial losses because he would be more than compensated by follow-up production orders and by payments for a Pentagon-dictated design change initiated over the contract's life. Second, the TPP assumed an omniscience on the part of those in "McNamara's band" to forecast the future defense needs of the United States over too long a time.

No one looking ahead could have been that smart. In the face of the New Bureaucracy's absolute certitude, however, normal bureaucratic and congressional criticism was stifled, and control over the Defense Department's actions was left almost completely in the hands of McNamara and his appointees. Thus virtually no one questioned decisions that would have been subject to thoroughgoing review and required strict accounting in terms of results before the advent of the New Bureaucracy.

McNamara, the living symbol of the New Bureaucracy's arrogance toward the career public service, and his retinue have left the federal government, but their influence lives on. The Old Bureaucracy has taken their quasi-scientific notions of cost-effectiveness and cost-benefit techniques and exploited them for its own purposes, which has inhibited President Nixon in his attempts to decentralize and reduce the scope of the federal government's operations. It is a curious situation in that the procedures initially foisted on the career bureaucrats as the "modern, scientific management" way to insure necessary change are now being used by them to prevent reforms made necessary by those very procedures. This demonstrates the normal bureaucratic tendency to lay low and avoid attracting attention to one's own inadequacies, particularly when there is the likelihood of a search for those responsible for the U.S. involvement in Vietnam. Because of the military failure, no bureaucratic element of the executive branch wants its actions examined by Congress or the public. So, since 1969, Nixon's efforts to effect real change in a wide variety of areas have been thwarted on the specious grounds that programs in each of these areas are being administered by Cabinet departments more efficiently than ever before.

What has happened, of course, is that by playing McNamara's efficiency numbers game, the bureaucracy has been able to avoid having results compared with the stated objectives of the government's programs—that is, it has avoided a measurement of its effectiveness. The main difference between efficiency and effectiveness is that the latter includes an evaluation in relation to some overall goal, whereas efficiency is measured only in terms of the number of actions completed. For example, such a McNamarian measure of productivity as the "body count" in Vietnam did not indicate anything about the appropriateness of the activity itself. This obsession with productivity blinded us to the question of whether a given program was effective in terms of its effect on the war's outcome.

Since McNamara's departure from the Department of Defense, the career bureaucrats have taken his notion of "the more the better" and run with it. Status, promotions, and the number of one's subordinates depend on the ability to increase the number of requisitions filled, letters answered, persons added to the welfare rolls or passed through training programs, and so forth. In such a system it becomes increasingly difficult to change, modify, or drop a program; almost anything will be continued that can be presented cleverly and with assurance. As a result, temporary political appointees to high-level positions in the federal bureaucracy more often than not find themselves called upon to merely sanction programs already underway instead of introducing innovations, even if a specific program has been discredited by an internal evaluation.

This should come as no surprise, because those who sought to gain control over the bureaucratic world after the military failure in Vietnam overestimated their capacity to influence a stubborn political reality: that to stop or change what the government is actually doing in any area is to acknowledge and draw attention to past mistakes. Because almost everyone in public life is burdened with skeletons from their past, professional bureaucrats, especially those who claim the general title of "administrator," have been able to play on their political mentors' fears and lack of certainty about the shape of the solutions they want for America's domestic and national problems.

The worst thing about the administrative Brahmins' ability to manipulate their political mentors is the increased sense of frustration it has incurred in the overall bureaucracy, which is already tormented with serious operational, morale, and philosophical difficulties. An example was the inability of President Nixon to get Congress to agree to consolidate the many scattered federal manpower programs into a single program under which the Secretary of Labor would dispense federal funds to governors and mayors. Those in the bureaucracy who believed that such an action was long overdue and who had worked to bring it about were dismayed by the action of the Senate-House Conference committee, which rejected the President's plan and not only kept all the programs but raised their number from fourteen to twenty-two. They concluded, and rightly so, that their commitment was not only futile but counterproductive.

The congressional involvement with the bureaucratic administrators is not widely recognized, but—like the interaction between lobbyists and members of Congress—it serves to perpetuate the status quo. The young deputy assistant secretary who takes office armed with his ideals, his autographed picture of the President, a personal flag, and a chair he is entitled to keep when he returns to wherever he came from (usually in fourteen to sixteen months) is no match for the bureaucratic administrators, who are not unlike convicts serving a life term who have become trusties in a well-regulated prison. In recent years few political appointees have been able to break through the insulation placed around their activities by career diplomats with an administrative axe to grind. As a consequence, negative control over entire departments in the executive branch (such as HEW, Labor, Defense, and HUD) has come to be vested in the hands of those with no real operational responsibilities for results from action programs. HEW is a good case in point; Robert Finch gave up in utter frustration after two years of attempting to get the administrative Brahmins to do something more than to tell him why something couldn't be done. It's a world where new ideas are always suspect, and usually opposed, for no better reason than they are not in the regulations.

The bureaucratic malaise that has beset the federal government since the military failure in Vietnam is likely to worsen. There is no assurance that any reform—structural or otherwise—

can be instituted that will not be sabotaged by those with a vested interest in maintaining the status quo. The irony is that most of the career civil servants who went to Washington hoping to have an influence on the vital issues facing the United States have come to realize that the programs and policies they worked to develop have not helped much at all. They also know that the job for which they are best rewarded is the one that is efficiently pursued to an ineffective conclusion. Problems are not solved. In fact, whole careers are precisely based on not solving problems but on perpetuating an endless cycle: view with great concern, study the problem, evaluate the study, debate the study's evaluation, concede the necessity for a "pilot project," and then restudy the problem until there are so many solutions that "the" problem becomes one of evaluating the solutions rather than solving the problem. If this seems farfetched, consider what the term "quality education" has come to mean in terms of the programs, problems, and solutions being considered to achieve it.

The bureaucrat who has concluded that there is little he can do to change things, or even to minimize the mistakes of others, is not much different than his counterpart in the private sector. Both display a studied indifference to the exhortations of persons with a public image to protect—or build—who call upon them to break a trail into a New Frontier, lay bricks in a Great Society, or meet the social responsibility of business. They were believers who have become disillusioned by the disparity between public rhetoric and actual practice, and are now nine-to-five skeptics. And Vietnam is at the root of the discontent of these hitherto hard-working "get on with the job" bureaucrats, who literally are the backbone of our government. They have taken the measure of U.S. leadership—in and out of the bureaucratic world—and have found it wanting in courage, integrity, and basic competence. Consequently, they have withdrawn their "above and beyond" active support of the present-day leadership until it changes its ways because they have lost confidence in the meaning and purpose of their life's work. Theirs is a sabotage of spirit. Yet the administrative Brahmins, who constantly wail for a return to the "good old days" when people worked overtime for no extra compensation or time off, are the first ones out of government-subsidized parking lots at five o'clock, on their way to Washington's noninvolved suburbs.

In the years since Vietnam the working bureaucracy of the federal government has become America's most silent minority. Vietnam is the *bête noire* of their existence because it has prevented an objective consideration of the real problems of government.

One of the prime effects of our military failure is that it has left the federal government singularly unprepared to resolve the harsh economic dilemmas revealed as a result of our overlong involvement in the war. What makes the economic situation especially difficult is that there is widespread congressional and public resistance not only to raising taxes but to cutting federal spending of any kind, defense or domestic, which poses a special problem for the politician-statesman. If he defines the problems broadly they will be rejected by the taxpaying public on the grounds that the cost is too great, and if defined narrowly the crisis will seem fragmented and merely shift from one area to another. If he establishes goals and priorities on a broadly based notion of the American Dream they will be rejected by the greatly expanded interest-group pluralism that has emerged since the Vietnam War, and if he establishes specific, categorical goals, they will become a victim of the pulling and hauling among the competing interest groups.

Implicit in this discussion about the "cautious government" is the question of how it can resolve the classic liberal dilemma of majority rule versus minority rights and take the actions required to address problems caused by, or at least deferred by, the war. In the past, it has usually been possible to achieve a consensus among the power bases of government and bring about reasonably balanced social, political, and economic change through the interactions of various interest groups. Today, however, the situation is considerably different because the number of interest groups has proliferated and splintered to such an extent that the conventional bases of political power—that is, those within the Congress and the executive branch—don't know which way to turn in order to get broad public support. This has left the individual legislator whose continued re-election is dependent upon the consistent voting support of an ethnic, religious, or economic bloc in a serious bind. He is no longer able to appeal to interest groups as such because the claims and expectations *within* each of these groups are often mutually exclusive. As a result, government programs have been directed toward whichever interest group has appeared to speak for the broadest category of persons at any given time. This tends to short-change important segments of society such as blacks, militant youth, and members of unorganized labor because they are grossly underrepresented in prevailing interest groups.

In the face of an increasing babble from competing groups concerning the direction, speed, and methods of change, government leaders have retreated behind a wall of bureaucratic conservatism erected by career bureaucrats, a condition that is likely to continue as long as the war and its emotional aftermath prevent an objective evaluation of national priorities. Thus the authority of government based on the consent/support of the governed has been replaced by the arbitrary authority of the bureaucracy to rule by regulation rather than by law, and the bureaucracy, with its current rejection of ideology and its acceptance of perverse pragmatism, only acts—and then grudgingly—to facilitate previously mandated change when it is pressed to do so by an interest group strong enough to make the point stick.

The federal government will not meet the overdue legitimate needs of our society until its political leadership provides the ideological authority and structure with which to pass judgment on the deliberately destructive policies of the Vietnam War, a fundamentally political task that must start with the reclamation of government control from the wasteland of bureaucratic indifference. Today, voters are almost completely turned off by the political process, having lost all hope of having any control over their so intensely admired democratic system.

An example of the kind of thing that has turned off the electorate is that although the results of the 1968 and 1972 presidential primaries revealed unexpectedly large constituencies for candidates promising major change, the House of Representatives—which has the sole responsibility for originating the many bills to pay for the war—has remained largely unresponsive to the turmoil in national and international politics caused by the U.S. involvement in Vietnam.

The American people have developed a strange new political psychology because of what they perceive as the government's indifference to the painful reality of the consequences of the war: their trust in their government and its institutions has been replaced by cynicism. They see an acknowledgment by Congress and the executive branch of the need for solutions to the nation's overwhelming domestic problems—problems that have been made much worse by the financial and psychological pressure brought on by the Vietnam War—as meaningless when the lion's share of U.S. tax dollars has gone to the war, to the inflated defense establishment, and to special interests, and when the federal bureaucracy is concerned only with maintaining the status quo rather than actually dealing with these problems. The public wonders how it can support a government that is either incredibly unrealistic, inept, or hypocritical—or all three.

The government, not surprisingly, does not see it this way, and its spokesmen—both elected and appointed—have launched a multipronged verbal search-and-destroy assault against its critics in an effort to obscure its nonperformance. Thus another result of widespread public disillusionment with government—and the refusal of critics to stop asking embarrassing questions—will be the use of government to restrict personal freedom. Beginning with the Johnson administration there has been in process the transferral of responsibility for the failure in Vietnam from those who masterminded the policies to the disenchanted, carping critics—liberal and conservative—who have come to see that politics in twentieth-century America has become the art of the implausible and ineffective. During eight years of war, administration spokesmen have so persistently blamed and browbeaten those who have sought genuine structural reform of the government that they are now prime candidates to be the objects of any recriminations about the whole Vietnam ordeal.

The result of this pursuit of orthodoxy is not difficult to predict. As one after another federal "bold experiment" comes a cropper anyone who has criticized the government will become the target of ordinary citizens, pressure groups, and politicians in need of symbolic scapegoats. As fear is spread by those with a personal vested interest in silencing all criticism, dissenters will sink lower and lower in esteem, until all who seek real change in the American system will be more disliked than any other group in society. The general public will become aroused by what they consider the arrogance and insubordination of these critics, who will be variously called anarchists, communists, outside agitators, or elitist intellectuals.

Congress will respond by organizing more and more special investigative commissions, passing stringent laws governing the dissenting minority's behavior and curtailing the rights and privileges of those who see Congress as nothing more than a group of political hacks looking for scapegoats to avoid their responsibilities.

The career men in the federal bureaucracy, characteristically, will withhold funds not only from groups lacking political clout but from those who are declared to be the enemies of democracy. The bureaucrats will become even more powerful; no matter who the president, he will be increasingly dependent on their support to maintain the "mystery, rules, and authority" of the American political system. In consolidating their gains, the entire governmental bureaucratic structure will be centralized to a degree that would have seemed impossible a few years ago and unflinching allegiance will be demanded from elected and appointed officials alike. The bureaucracy will weaken and manipulate appointed political leaders by circumventing them on significant issues on the grounds that the issues are strictly operational matters and that the leaders should be concerned only with policy.

The bureaucratic Brahmins can be counted upon to undermine their two principal critics—the President and the electorate —by pitting them against each other, especially with proposals for "public" participation in executive decision making, and they will promote an environment of secrecy to reinforce their authoritarianism. Further, they will restrict other bureaucrats, who previously had operational responsibilities for programs, through the "principle of accountability," making them quieter, more reasonable, and more careful. Thus the remainder of the federal bureaucracy, both civilian and military, will become afraid and passive at a time of fundamental realignment and redefinition of actual political power.

While there is no sure way to prevent the emergence of the American Bureaucratic State, there are steps that concerned citizens ought to take.

First, we must recognize that the government today is more like a diversified conglomerate corporation than a community of persons organized to limit the role of government to those functions necessary to protect the individual and his property. The public must make clear what it believes government can and cannot do and should and should not do. The realization that there is a class of problems over which government can have little or no formal control would save us much time, energy, and unnecessary disappointment.

Second, we must make sure that our public servants are not allowed to become a kind of priesthood by adopting some objective criteria regulating their selection, whether they are appointed, elected, or part of the career bureaucracy.

Third, we need to emphasize areas of national agreement and stop bickering over means where the ends are agreed upon. We must resist all efforts to make us support special interests at the expense of others by becoming more sensitive to "prestige" programs promoted by a restive bureaucracy.

As a consequence of our failure in Vietnam we are confronted with a crisis of confidence in our government, and crisis, as the Chinese emphasize, entails both danger and opportunity. We can either constructively work to turn this crisis to our advantage or let it get out of hand, thus threatening our democratic form of government. We must restructure the government to meet the needs of a changing technological and international environment or it is certain that it will be restructured for us by those in positions of bureaucratic power and influence.

SEVEN

The People

"If a vocal minority, however fervent its cause, prevails over reason and the will of the majority, this nation has no future as a free society. Let historians not record that when America was the most powerful nation in the world we passed on the other side of the road and allowed the last hopes for peace and freedom of millions of people to be suffocated by the forces of totalitarianism. And so tonight—to you, the great silent majority of my fellow Americans—I ask for your support."
—Richard M. Nixon
November 3, 1969

THE AMERICAN people's initial reaction to the end of America's longest and most unpopular war was a vast collective sigh of relief. But after the prisoners are no longer newsworthy and we are no longer bombing our presumptive enemies in Southeast Asia, what will happen? Will there be profound psychic damage? Vindictive second thoughts? A hunt for scapegoats? Or would we who in the past have known only America the Invincible shrug off the failure? Would we accept a Communist Indochina as something inevitably cast up by the wave of the future rather than a consequence of America's involvement in the Vietnam War? Would we, as a people, agree with the left intellectuals that Communism offers the best hope for the successful rehabilitation of a battered Vietnam?

Nobody can be sure what the answers to these questions will be once the fact of the U.S. military failure in Vietnam has been finally and completely acknowledged. One can only surmise, based upon how the American people perceived and responded to the war and to the startling revelations of widespread ineptitude on the part of those with national political responsibilities. Therefore our reflections will concentrate on what we have learned and observed about the place and functions of the American people in the Vietnam War and about the fateful role of those who actually fought the war.

There are some ground rules to this chapter that should be mentioned. The overwhelming majority of the population was either actively anti-war or passively supportive of government policies. Although these groups could be broken down demographically, we are limiting ourselves to the following categories in our discussion: (1) youth (the "under-thirty" generation) who were against the war; (2) youth who were not necessarily against the war but who were affected by it; (3) adults who were against the war; (4) adults who were passively supportive of government policies; and (5) Vietnam veterans, who were affected by the war in a special way.

Also, it is assumed that any critique of America's post-war role and social conditions must include an assessment of the effect of that role and those conditions upon the ideological conditions and tensions of our time. Finally, if we are to transcend the trauma of our military failure, the influence of others' insights into the delusions that led us into the war are now part of our burden. We must attempt to understand those delusions, and if we do, then we are faced with new tasks—namely, those connected with structural reform of our government and the necessity to change the methods by which we select our political leaders and give them the authority to make decisions such as those that led us into the Vietnam quagmire.

Today's youth grew up badly scarred by a succession of unpopular wars and interventions, assassinations, riots, violent confrontations, and an ever-present "Consciousness I" mentality that could enable us—and others—to destroy not only each other but the entire world. All of this was further aggravated by the Vietnam War, which has made America an evil country in the eyes of many of its own people and has afflicted many of our youth with a pessimism unconditioned by a sense of balance gained from earlier events. Thus, young people tend to see U.S. affairs in a different light and from a much different perspective than their elders.

Since the beginnings of America's ground-combat involvement in Vietnam in early 1965, the attitude of those youth who were opposed to the war veered from what Max Weber has called the "ethic of responsibility" to the "ethic of absolute ends." The ethic of responsibility, in this case, was set forth by successive Democratic and Republican administration spokesmen who warned of the dire consequences to ourselves and others if we did not take an active role in Southeast Asia, with an implicit acknowledgment that it might be necessary to compromise our fundamental values by maintaining a dictatorship in South Vietnam in order to achieve a presumed good—the prevention of a Chinese takeover of Southeast Asia.

At first many young people rejected this view of responsibility—which was inherited from preceding generations—on philosophical grounds; then, particularly on college campuses, they tended to shift to a passively negative attitude and finally to active physical opposition to the war on the grounds that there was a marked discrepancy between the stated objectives of the U.S. involvement in South Vietnam and the actual political systems and conditions in that artificially created country. This shift to the ethic of absolute ends has been one of the most confusing aspects of the Vietnam War because it was based more on the symbolism of the war than on its actual facts. In other words, college-educated youth tended to use the war as a means to challenge the discrepancy between the larger values of the American system and its various subgroups (the church, political parties, the business, education, and military establishments, the liberal intellectuals) and the actual practices of the society. They used their opposition to the war to gain widespread public attention, but the war was never their basic concern.

Within this group there was a radical minority who thrived on the war and its prolongation and used their ostensible anti-war orientation to radicalize other young people and to undermine authority. This minority got the headlines and arrogated unto itself the spokesman role for all youth who opposed the war. Concern about the moral issue of using death and destruction for political purposes dominated their rhetoric, but overall they displayed an almost total lack of understanding about the complex issues involved, nor did they offer suggestions about how to end the war that would not have left us with even greater problems in Vietnam and at home.

These young people should be given credit as being the first to realize that the United States had failed in Vietnam to do with military power what it had set out to do and make this failure a prominent issue in their protests. But once they found out that the public wasn't very interested and the government wouldn't listen, they used protest about the war for other purposes, largely unrelated to the war itself. We may also conclude that only a minuscule proportion of youth opposed the war on strictly moral grounds. For example, one theme that emerged from their variegated protests was that social and economic programs at home were being short-changed to pay for the war's rapidly escalating costs. However, the antics of the Yippies *et al.* obscured their arguments and alienated those persons in and out of government who might have been able to bring pressure to end the war.

The ultimate irony of their protest, however, is that it was aimed at the wrong audience. As we have noted, the active antiwar group never constituted more than a slender minority of the under-thirty population. If they had been able to convince their peers who were not necessarily in favor of the war to join them in solid opposition to the government's Vietnam policies rather than trying to change the minds of the status quo authorities, they would certainly have been more effective. In short, because they protested to the wrong audience and because their protests displayed no understanding of the structural and institutional ways in which our nation deals with high-level policies, they tended to generate a lot of sound and fury that ultimately signified very little.

The consequences of our military failure upon these young

people are predictably bad. Because they did not succeed in influencing national policy they have become badly disillusioned with the entire democratic process. They seem, as a result, to have rejected any sense of responsibility toward trying to influence American foreign policy on either pragmatic or ideological grounds, and now profess an aversion and indifference to doing so. The effect of this basically conservative reaction will not be a simple one, especially as those who have dominated policy in the United States for the past two decades are replaced by those who have come of political age during the Vietnam War.

In contrast to the activist attitudes and behavior of the young people who were against the war stand those of the preponderant majority of youth who were passive about it, but their approval of the government's war policies was more tacit than real. They did not rush to the recruiting stations to support either Johnson's or Nixon's policies, and as long as they were able to avoid military service by one means or another, the war appeared at least necessary in their eyes. Without belaboring the point unduly, it is not inaccurate to say that the Vietnam War's unpopularity is better gauged by the overwhelming number of physically and academically qualified American youth who quietly opted to avoid military duty during the war rather than by the much smaller number who noisily protested against the war.

Those youth who *avoided* personal involvement in the war differed substantially from those who *evaded* the war; the latter used illegal means while the former used the many loopholes in the draft law, which was stacked in such a way that those who were affluent and influential enough were able to miss the war entirely. The avoiders' response to our military failure in Vietnam has been to treat it as a self-fulfilling justification for their actions. Their curious logic holds that because they were for the war, however passively, their personal noninvolvement absolves them from any responsibility for the subsequent failure and its consequences to the United States and its institutions. It is not wholly surprising that this group of young people should yield to moods of alienation and rejection of one sort or another. It has happened before, but never so pervasively or with such damaging effects. It is one thing for them to claim a lack of responsibility for our military failure, but in doing so these young people have given up on the idea of representative government and rejected the efforts of those who have attempted to defend that idea.

Perhaps the ultimate consequence of our military failure upon the majority of our youth is the impetus it has given to an almost compulsive revival of ethnicity. The indicators are there: a growing wrath about both the social and the real dollar costs, as well as the opportunities lost, that they are expected to bear in pursuit of Great Society egalitarianism while we are still paying for the Vietnam War. Not anger, wrath. Call them Middle America, the silent majority, hard hats—but every attempt to promote egalitarian objectives at their expense feeds the fires on the right. To date these young persons don't have a coherent means by which to express their wrath, but it is potent enough to give birth to a new political alliance between them and those adults who feel imperiled by the liberal intellectuals' denunciation of their social, economic, cultural, and religious value systems. If large-scale unemployment and/or a protracted recession should follow the end of our involvement in Vietnam there is scant doubt that a large majority of the youth who were not against the war would be in the forefront of a right-wing-inspired search for exculpation of the sins, causes, and persons presumed to be responsible for their condition. The groping dissatisfaction of youth with the present system is so general that only the catalyst of involuntary unemployment is needed to precipitate a major crisis of confidence in the American system.

Interestingly, the reaction of both the actively anti-war and the more passive youth groups is essentially the same: a feeling of alienation from the establishment and a lack of responsibility for the war or its damaging effects on U.S. society. They seem disinterested in constructively challenging—or even encouraging—the status quo forces to make necessary structural reforms in the military, in social or economic institutions, or in the political arena, their abortive efforts to restructure the 1972 Democratic presidential nominating convention notwithstanding; when it came time to *vote* in the 1972 elections, only 40 per cent of the registered voters under the age of twenty-five showed up at the polls, as compared with 60 per cent of their elders. The argument that this dismal showing was a result of an unwillingness to indulge in the "lesser of two evils" presidential-candidate game has little merit, because it overlooks the fact that young people also neglected to vote in the local and state contests, thereby enabling the entrenched forces to stay in power by default and leaving those more progressive candidates who were counting on the "youth vote" with nothing but campaign debts.

This shunning of the hard pragmatism of electoral politics is likely to discourage many potentially reformist candidates from even running for office. If only youth was willing to get up off its collective rear end and work to support those who might make a difference in fighting the seemingly overwhelming battles against pollution, overpopulation, racism, militarism, religious intolerance, and sexual and national chauvinism, we might begin to see some real progress.

By their attitudes, young people have an immediate effect on what happens next, because just as nature abhors a vacuum so do those who seek political power. And these politicians have been able to exploit youth's indifference about who directs the government in such a way as to leave the destinies of America in the hands of an insignificant minority. Youth is much less a *force* for a movement toward the political right than it is a negatively positive influence on this trend, in that its underinvolvement in electoral politics automatically advances the policies of the right. Youth apparently couldn't care less whether their or anyone else's civil rights are abridged as long as their life style is not materially affected. They seem not to care whether the elusive concepts of political freedom are sacrificed on the altar of political expediency.

These are not pleasant conclusions. However, because our youth has for the past decade demonstrated a penchant for self-indulgence it seems they might accept the notion of political purges as a substitute for individual responsibility. It is worth noting that youth's *modus operandi* is judgment without involvement, buttressed by a feeling that their presumed moral superiority is sufficient to preclude any adverse judgment about their sincerity—the kind of attitude that in the past led to the Salem witchcraft trials and McCarthyism. This alienation and indifference represents an explicit denial of Charles Reich's thesis that the "youth revolution" is trying to make America livable. Instead of passing on to "Consciousness III," where they will stop consuming what they don't need, doing meaningless work, and playing ego games, young people have passed on to a higher order of indifference, where they refuse to try to bring about needed change because of others' past failures. Youth's emotional and physical aloofness from present-day realities contains the seeds for the destruction of the life style they have adopted as part of their deliberate isolationism. Sooner or later, history imposes itself upon those who interpret it to justify their own present and future inaction.

The sadness one feels in all this is that youth has lost its sense of direction and proportion about the old American ideals revolving around democracy, social justice, and brotherhood. The war is their excuse, but it is not sufficient reason for them to throw up their hands in despair about all public wrongs. By their very indifference, intolerance, and lack of real involvement, young people are likely to make worse the social problems cited most frequently in their arguments against the war. This is not to deny the validity of some of their complaints, but only to emphasize again that by turning away they are giving support to a regressive, restrictive status quo. A prime consequence of our military failure is that youth has lost its dynamism, its sense of progress, and there is probably going to be a period of extraordinary social regression, as a minority of reactionary activists take up the slack left by youth's abandonment of its progressive ideals.

Adults against the war were always an extremely small percentage of the total over-thirty population. They were a much less homogenous group than the anti-war youth group, which was principally made up of college students; they included persons from almost every background, from members of the Cath-

olic clergy to corporate executives to housewives whose previous
political activism was negligible. This is not to say they did not
have their share of "knee-jerk liberals" or that they did not differ
over tactics, over what it was that was wrong, or over how the
war got started and why, but that they were in substantial agreement that continuation of the war was a terrible mistake for
the United States.

One notable exception to this kind of personal outlook was
that of Martin Luther King, who was very explicit in making
connections between the war and its damaging effects on U.S.
domestic problems and racism. Although Dr. King opposed all
war because of his belief in nonviolence, his opposition to the
Vietnam War was as much pragmatic as it was moral. Other
black leaders followed Dr. King's lead and kept themselves and
their organizations outside the main thrust of the national anti-
war movement, insofar as there was one. Black opposition to the
war, from both youth and adults, generally remained consistent
with Dr. King's views; except for a brief flurry of concern in 1968
over the disproportionate number of black combat casualties, the
war never really excited the black community as a practical issue.*

Throughout the long and divisive debate over the Vietnam
War the anti-war adults succeeded where the youth had failed.
They knew how to contact congressmen and influence their local
communities, and—most importantly—they were voters and knew
how to finance campaigns. They were able to present a sharp
dilemma to President Johnson: get out of Vietnam or get out of
office. But theirs was not an easy success. They grew weary in
their long fight, and the consequences of our military failure
greatly affected their emotional well-being and willingness to
continue in an activist role in the post-Vietnam period.

As a result, their future response to the problems revealed
and caused by our involvement in Vietnam will command less
and less of their personal attention, and they will probably re-

---

* See *Promise or Peril*, especially Chapter 5, for a discussion of the
form and substance of black college youths' opposition to the war.

vert to being relatively uninvolved private citizens. They may still be interested in how post-war problems are approached, but as long as apparently moderate solutions are adopted there seems little chance they will continue as an active political force in any coherent, organized way. Some can be counted upon to pursue whatever cause appears popular, but these "automatic activists" were never a large part of the overall group.

Adults against the war were effective because they understood the nuances of power and focused on a single issue. Now they apparently feel that the basis for their political activism has ended. This is unfortunate because their withdrawal removes an enlightened and effective group from the active political process and tends to let government be dominated by bureaucratic technicians. Perhaps they will be persuaded by the force of subsequent events to stay in the mainstream of political involvement as the consequences of our military failure run their course, but one must doubt it because of the general apathy surrounding today's political issues and debate. Economics has replaced politics as the rallying point.

Those adults who were not necessarily against the war but were affected by it are largely members of a group that is often called the Great Silent Majority. These are people who have always tended to shun active participation in broad political, social, and economic issues but who nevertheless have provided the great bulk of money and manpower to carry out our nation's social, political, and military adventures. On the one hand, this group is derided for its lack of sympathy with less fortunate citizens and for refusing to examine or question the choices made by America's governing elite. On the other hand, it is exalted by that elite as being the most important force in the political decision-making process.

During the course of writing this book I interviewed several hundred persons who can be considered bona fide members of the Great Silent Majority. The persons I talked to were not at the bottom of the social and income scale; they were stable breadwinners, churchgoers, voters, family men and women. About one-fourth had completed college and slightly fewer than two out of five had some education beyond high school. One out of three of the men were veterans of World War II, the Korean War, or peacetime service prior to 1960. Generally, they had achieved their positions in life through hard work and, sometimes, bitter sacrifices. They have strong opinions about the war and its aftereffects, but are not inclined to join politically active organizations that reflect their views. Many do not like the present political order, which seems to emphasize war and welfare, but they go along with it because of their family responsibilities —and because they aren't sure how they would fare if America's political system swung to either the extreme right or left.

The interviews were conducted by means of a coordinated series of questions and discussion topics followed by informal— but structured—conversation to discover the underlying meaning of their responses. Although my inquiry ranged beyond trying to assess their reaction to the fact of our military failure in Vietnam —which, however, I had to treat not as a fact but as an untested hypothesis—I will limit my discussion here to that part of their responses. The consistency of the answers to my questions throughout the sample suggests that it is possible to generalize from those answers about the overall attitudes of the Great Silent Majority.

As background, I should state that as a group these people have been highly influenced by the notion propagated by America's war culture that the United States has a special obligation to defend the bad from the worse, anywhere in the world. Further, they believe that their personal status is intertwined with their country's military prowess and is dependent upon their support of the governing elite in its war-making decisions. Their attitude toward our military failure was related to their sense of their own—or their family's—involvement in the war; as is true with a large number of social beliefs, one's attitude toward a nation at war is often grounded in one's attitude toward one's self.

It was obvious that our military failure was personally painful to this group, and they tended either to avoid dealing with it, to see only those aspects of it that they wanted to see, or to find scapegoats, a common reaction when a nation's people must account not for its strength but its weakness. How they actually did this gives us an insight into their attitudes about the war's outcome. First, they tried to excuse our poor showing in Vietnam by insisting that it would not have been so bad if only "they" (those who opposed the war) had been whipped into line and had not been allowed to give "aid and comfort" to the enemy. Further, they insulated themselves by limiting their outlook and range of comparisons in such a way as to avoid examining the difference between the government's official rhetoric and the actual results of its policy in Vietnam. Then, in an attempt to reduce the impact of our military failure, they denied its importance, not in the sense that not winning a war is a trivial matter but that this was not really an important war. Finally, their attitude was one of resignation, a reluctant acceptance that it is our fate to be deceived by our allies.

When comparing their individual support—however each person defined it—of the war effort with that of others, they tended to point with pride to the achievement of a son or other relative who had served in the war rather than to anything they themselves had done—except pay their taxes and not complain. But satisfaction with one's self and one's friends depends on seeing some merit in one's contribution vis-à-vis those who worked for and supported the war on a higher level of personal effort and sacrifice. At first, this seemed difficult for those whose participation in the Vietnam War had been only vicarious, but in many simple ways it was done. For example, many felt they had made a greater contribution to the war effort by virtue of their vocal hostility toward those who actively opposed it than had those who actually fought the war and were then disillusioned by their experience.

They also felt morally superior to those who opposed the war in that they felt their tacit support was in tune with the "American way," one of whose tenets is that the decision to make war is based upon spiritual and moral righteousness. They derived considerable satisfaction from their identification with the going social order, and regarded the views and decisions of the governing elite as appropriate to the situation—a sort of "father knows best" attitude. Thus in justifying their own lack of a passionately felt conviction about the war—pro or con—my respondents sometimes implied that "if it had been up to me, I—like you—would have told them not to get involved in the stupid war." They further rationalized their lack of involvement and concern in two ways: that they did not have enough information to know what was really best or to understand the politics of the war, and that they were generally indifferent to the war's effect on their lives. They seemed to feel that because one man could not make a difference there was no need to try.

Like any findings on the nature of men's social attitudes and beliefs, even in such a culture-bound inquiry as this one, the information gathered suggests certain theoretical propositions that may be incorporated into the main body of political theory dealing with the relation between man and the state, especially when the state is at war. Let us consider five such propositions and one tentative hypothesis more or less growing out of my interviews.

1. When a nation is at war there is great social, economic, and political pressure on the people of that nation to support its war effort. This in turn puts an equal pressure on the individuals of that society to rationalize their support and therefore the war itself.

2. The greater the threat to the individual's self-esteem posed by his support of the war, the greater is his need to rationalize the belief that what he is doing is needed by his nation.

3. The more completely a society accepts the rationalization of the war, the more it demands that *all* the people offer total support. One psychological result of this build-up of pressure is that if the war is not successfully concluded, those who supported it can justify their support by blaming the failure on those who did not. I hold that this belief in the rightness of supporting the state at war is one that has always been held by the silent—and sometimes by the not-so-silent—majority in the United States throughout its history, and probably throughout most of the rest of the world as well.

4. The more a society insists—through political propaganda,

the development of new threats, and deficit financing—upon continued support for the war, the more will social dissatisfaction be channeled into intraclass rivalry instead of interclass resentment and conflict.

5. As a corollary to the preceding point, the longer this support is demanded, the more the broad mass of people will focus upon the physical aspects of their participation rather than its ideological elements.

We come, finally, to a hypothesis that arises from our inquiry into the consequences of military failure but that goes much beyond the range of this book, and I mention it here speculatively, undogmatically, even regretfully: The ideals of the American Revolution—liberty and equality—are often called into play by the governing elite when a nation is at war, because they are useful in serving the government's need for freedom of political action at that time. These are potent ideals, and they have an autonomy of their own even if the forces that promulgate them decline in strength. Over the long run, however, they become little more than myths if they are not actively supported by some major stratum of society. It is clear that neither the present governing elite in the United States nor the Great Silent Majority has much affection for these ideals as guiding principles aside from their expedient rhetorical value in proclaiming "victory" and "peace with honor."

So far, Vietnam veterans have been generally apolitical in their outlook and behavior, but this may change if they feel compelled to become aggressive in defense of their actions in the war. If they are blamed for our military failure, they may respond violently, as a group. This blame does not have to be explicitly verbalized to produce an anti-social response; it can be expressed in terms of the treatment the veterans receive from the government and from individual citizens, which can make the veterans feel they are being punished or blamed for our military failure, whether the rest of us consciously think this or not.

Few persons are aware of just how psychologically fragile the veterans are and that the condition is not confined to those who saw active combat duty. It seems as if their observation of the effect of the U.S. presence on the Vietnamese people themselves is as much a cause of their emotional disturbance as physical combat. The veterans are bewildered over what they have done and seen, and its meaning in their lives, and it is much more complicated than the conventional post-combat culture shock that occurs when a serviceman re-enters civilian life.

Basically this bewilderment derives from the veterans' recognition that the officially proclaimed unbroken string of U.S. military successes in the Vietnam War added up to a military failure. To them it seemed that the more successful we said we were, the stronger the enemy became. They find it hard to believe that anyone in a responsible position could not have known how badly and wastefully the war was being run, and to so little purpose. They feel they were played for suckers and that they are taking the brunt of everyone's frustration about the war.

They reject the American military system because they see it as incompetent and run by fools or knaves. They have no sense of idealism about their military experience and little empathy for the branch of the service in which they served, their organization or unit, or even their former comrades. In fact, their attitude is best described as one of hostility toward the military system for not being able to bring them home "winners." They have yet to really raise the "what went wrong and why" question, but their present alienation and despair can easily turn, or be turned by others, into violently expressed anger.

These attitudes are a direct consequence of our military failure, and unless they can be modified or changed they spell long-range trouble for the nation. We cannot count on the veterans, as a group, to support such military activities as service in the reserve programs or in civilian military action programs. They have been turned off by their experience and it is going to take a great deal of effort to regain not only their support but the support of the young men who are now coming of age in any attempt to solve America's problems. We must eliminate them from being part of the problem before they can become part of the solution.

In each of the groups we have examined there has been a turning away from the consequences of our failure in Vietnam. This is similar to what has happened earlier in other countries, but we should keep in mind the fact that, unlike other nations that became mired in military failures, we *chose* to wage the Vietnam War with citizen soldiers—draftees—and as such "the people" cannot dissociate themselves from the outcome and its consequences.

EIGHT

The Economy

"The greatest changes are effected there without his con-
currence. . . . The condition of his village, the police of
his street, the repairs of the church or the parsonage do
not concern him; for he looks upon all these things as
unconnected and as the property of a powerful stranger
whom he calls the government."

—Alexis de Tocqueville

INFLATION, balance-of-payments deficits, lagging growth rates in
labor productivity, persistent unemployment, devaluation of the
U.S. dollar, a running battle between the President and the
Congress to get the latter to restore fiscal sanity and stop attempting to be all things to all men at all times: these are some
of the economic consequences directly attributable to our military
failure and to the costs of fighting and ending the Vietnam War.
It was not fought on the "cheap," but it *was* fought on credit.

The fiscal problems involved in the war go far beyond the
"guns versus butter" dilemma; as part of McNamara's and
Johnson's deception of Congress as to the real costs of the war,
we took care of neither guns nor butter. By April 1969, when
President Nixon opted to end the war, the costs of liquidating it
had reached a point where they were almost prohibitive, if he
still wanted to maintain a semblance of economic order and fiscal
responsibility. Between April 1969 and August 1971, when the
President announced Phase I of his Economic Stabilization
Program, the American economy literally was in defiance of conventional economic wisdom by being simultaneously in a state of

inflation and of recession. We should remember, although the signal has been lost in the noise surrounding the succeeding phases of the wage-price control program, that the immediate forcing factor was that the continued costs of fighting the Vietnam War had eroded international confidence in the dollar and that the goods-producing sector of our economy had lost much of its ability to compete with foreign-made products.

To a nation that identifies its well-being with a gargantuan, ever-growing Gross National Product and a continual export surplus, the inflation and recession that led to the August 1971 imposition of wage and price controls in "peacetime" is doubly ominous. On the one hand, the once positive notion of economic growth has taken on disturbing overtones because it, like the Vietnam War, appears to be beyond our capacity to manage without befouling the environment along the way. On the other hand, also like Vietnam, the concentrations of private economic power in the United States held by big business and labor unions have become so strong that they are insulated from normal government monetary and fiscal policies designed to prevent their activities from producing anti-social outcomes.

After more than a year of personal labor in trying to make the President's Economic Stabilization Program work, I could only conclude that the extent to which corporate power can be exercised for its own purposes is far greater than that of government to prevent it from exercising that power, and consequently to control and alter social outcomes. No organized corporate conspiracy is implied in this conclusion; it is just that the corporate sector was no more willing to sacrifice its profits to maintain the fiction of an independent democratic South Vietnam than the affluent members of the middle class were willing to sacrifice their sons' lives. As a result, the burden of fighting the war was shifted to those without wealth and influence, and the corporate sector's leadership shifted the unusual wage and income pressures generated by the war from themselves and their stockholders to the consumers.

Although Americans rarely think in such terms, perhaps the motivating force behind this shift is based on the fact that it can be justified in terms of the general public's lack of involvement with the real issues of war and peace. After all, why should a corporate officer worry about ripping off the government when he believes the bureaucracy is overpaid, America's overseas involvements are a joke, and his labor force is getting too large a share of his proceeds? All these feelings have been fed by the rapid income shifts caused by the Vietnam War. Why should he be concerned that his demands for special public benefits and subsidies exceed the revenue-raising ability of the government when the government's expenditures seem to bear no relation to domestic or international reality? The anticipated "peace dividend" following the end in Vietnam has evaporated because the costs of paying for the war and rebuilding the military establishment are greater than even the most optimistic estimates of a growth in the federal revenue.

These factors, which have come to the fore as a consequence of our military failure, aggravate the conflict among large, organized segments in the economy in their efforts to manipulate wages, prices, and productivity for narrow ends. The free-market model may still be the most appropriate standard by which to judge economic policies, but it is not as reliable as it once was because the rational quest for profits has been replaced by the exercise of arbitrary economic power. Organized labor must also share the responsibility with the military-industrial complex for taking advantage of the government's preoccupation with war and welfare to get theirs while the getting was good, which created the situation that led Nixon to experiment with wage-price controls.

After the war we probably will see more attempts at direct government intervention in the economy as a counterbalancing force in areas that seem to be especially subject to government influence and public pressure, but the government simply does not have the intellectual, emotional, or physical ability to carry out a successful "counterinflation" campaign against America's domestic "insurgents." According to Gardner Ackley, former chairman of President Johnson's Council of Economic Advisors, in the August 1972 *Review of Economics and Statistics,* "Recent experience with inflation has substantially heightened the sensitivity of most groups to actual or potential losses of relative position. For these reasons, there is a tendency to react more quickly, more fully, and frequently pre-emptively. *The more prompt and complete are the defensive reactions to inflation, the faster is its rate—that is, the more there is to defend against"* (italics added). Ackley also notes that business and union leaders are increasingly sophisticated about what they can get—and when.

The U.S. economy is extremely vulnerable to this kind of economic guerrilla warfare because none of the weapons available to the President to fight inflation is effective. It is true that the primary cause of inflation is government spending in excess of available revenues, usually as a result of fighting a war or stimulating the economy by one kind of pump priming or another, but these factors are now being intensified by corporations' and unions' market power, which is used to increase their real incomes at the expense of those with less power. Even if Nixon was able to get a balanced budget through Congress it is unlikely that the inflation-producing efforts to increase or protect income shares in the private sector would cease.

What this suggests is that the government will find itself engaged in a guerrilla war it can't win with the more powerful segments of the economy. The "enemy" has all the advantages because the executive branch must fight by the rules and cater to the legislative branch's tendency to honor the demands of its most favored constituents for special treatment.

Current U.S. inflation, caused in large part by the necessity of paying for the military debacle in Vietnam, which cost taxpayers approximately $250 billion, is the dominant social issue today. According to William Watts and Lloyd A. Free in *State of the Nation,* about 60 per cent of the public felt the country had lost ground in controlling inflation in the preceding year (1971); 55 per cent said they favored stricter price controls, but only 30 per cent wanted strengthened wage controls. This indicates that the public feels Phase II was ineffective in controlling the rate of inflation but that they nevertheless support more government intervention in areas controlled by the large and organized segments of the economy. But because most wage determinations are not made on the basis of collective bargaining, it appears that the general public endorses the somewhat fanciful notion of freely and competitively determined wages. In other words, the American people seem willing to embrace the idea of a controlled, regulated economy as long as they are permitted to continue their individual upward mobility. This is the siren song of fascism, the theme of which is that the middle and working classes are guaranteed financial security in exchange for giving up personal social and political freedoms. It has always been a bum deal, but people are inclined to go along until they realize— too late—that their freedom has been sacrificed for nothing.

Since the beginning of wage-price controls it has been clear to me that the people's acceptance of creeping fascism—that is, severe restrictions on their freedom in order to maintain their economic status and stability—is a direct result of the U.S. failure in Vietnam. They are mortally afraid of what rampant inflation can do to them because they know that the fragile social structure holding the country together could not survive the accompanying upheaval. So far (early 1973), the Nixon administration has resisted the temptation to use more overtly fascistic restrictions to alleviate the problem of inflation, but the pressures are bound to build over time as "structural" distortions in the economy become greater.

The government's problem is, first, that monetary and fiscal policies are uncontrollable and irresponsible because the Federal Reserve System acts as a law unto itself and the Congress attempts to be a universal paymaster to all men. Second, the powerful segments of the economy have enough economic and political leverage to avoid being brought to account for their excesses. And third, the American people are so skeptical, on the basis of past performance, of the government's ability to achieve its goals that they are unwilling to make personal sacrifices to achieve a social "good" such as a stable price level or full employment. Thus we have an impossible situation wherein the government is damned if it does and damned if it doesn't.

No one knows for sure what the government will do if inflation worsens, but it is clear that neither selective direct wage and price controls nor "voluntarism" is effective in controlling it and that the government's options in dealing with the problem are extremely limited. But it seems that, given the prevailing mood in the country, none of the government's arguments for restraint based upon "conscience" or the "rule of reason" will be taken seriously by participants in wage-price decisions. The "Why me?" response to a call for monetary sacrifices in the post-Vietnam era is likely to result in widespread evasion on the part of those with the power to do so and the application of political pressure by their advocates in the government to make sure the costs are borne by those without power—the poor, the sick, the aged—which is bound to produce strong anti-social reactions on the part of the powerless.

This, then, is perhaps the next-to-bottom-line consequence of the failure in Vietnam upon the American economy. I suspect that during the second Nixon administration there will be increasing pressures to institute even stricter direct controls over wage and price decisions than existed during World War II. The choice may well be between withdrawing subsidy support from such corporate cripples as Lockheed, Litton, and the "poor" farmers who receive billions of dollars for doing nothing or relying more heavily on government controls over private decision making. The odds-on choice favors the latter course—creeping fascism.

This does not mean that the government would directly undertake the production and distribution of goods and services, but that it would use controls over private decision making as the only way out of the dilemma caused by the conflict between private interests and the public interest, no matter how badly defined. The military failure in Vietnam exacerbated this situation because it raised fundamental questions about the values of the American society and about the nation's ability, as the richest, best educated, and most technically advanced in the world, to be all things to all men and nations simultaneously.

The war in Vietnam has been a multiple turning point and a shock to all established habits of political thinking. It placed a burden on the American people that few were prepared for; seldom have they been expected to support a war lacking real national purpose without understanding and accepting the fact that we simply did not know how to achieve victory. There are many explanations for the U.S. military failure in Vietnam (and many rationalizations for why it wasn't a failure), but the one I am going to offer will, I think, explain not only the military failure but failures in America's domestic, social, and environmental wars. I call it the "conflicting outcomes" theory, which holds that the application of the means and knowledge available to achieve a desirable, agreed-upon outcome in the environment of limited political-social-economic guerrilla type of war produces antinomical outcomes—that is, results contrary to those initially sought. These outcomes are as much a cause as they are an uncontrollable bad side effect of the technical difficulties of achieving desired objectives without producing different ones that no one wants. For example, it is difficult to design a political system that insures freedom for all and still encourages efficient, nonwasteful use of natural and economic resources. No one knows how to do it. The same can be said for creating a system of military security for those unable to defend themselves that maintains strong incentives for those expected to bear the physical burdens and sacrifices of providing that security. And for devising programs that allow genuine indigenous participation in decision making and yet insure the support of the American taxpayer, or that promote the healthy growth of former colonial peoples without encouraging (or at least not discouraging) additional political strife. No one is quite sure how to do any of these things.

Our reaction to the Vietnam War's conflicting outcomes set the pattern for approaching America's domestic "limited war" failures, particularly those calling for additional sacrifice or support from any significant portion of the population. It may very well be that because of our failure in Vietnam we will not be willing to try to develop the means and knowledge required to overcome our past failures and to avoid conflicting outcomes in the future. In this sense, Vietnam may be looked upon as an excuse not to attempt difficult problems even when it is clearly in our national interest to do so. It has made us gun-shy about facing problems that have the potential of producing conflicting outcomes. Two examples may suffice to make the point and indicate the application of the theory—the problems of poverty and pollution.

The issues are admittedly complex, and there may be conflicting outcomes that make the problem of poverty insoluble or at least place it beyond our capacity to solve without a major change in our institutional posture and personal outlook. However, there is no good reason for poverty to exist in the United States; the very poor are a small portion of the total population. The 1970 census data show that about 26 million people, or 13 per cent, have incomes below the government's official definition of poverty—slightly less than $4,000 per year for a family of four. Disregarding the argument about whether this level is too low, too high, or just right, to make up the difference between the incomes of the poor and the poverty level would take about $11 billion, or approximately 1 per cent of the Gross National Product. So why can't we just raise everyone up to the government's level and go on from there? Because, according to the theory of conflicting outcomes, the majority of the U.S. population does not want to—or at least not badly enough to make the necessary sacrifices.

Similarly, it was the considered judgment of those responsible for U.S. Vietnam policy to delay seeking a tax increase to pay for the war until it was too late to make a difference, on the grounds that most people did not want to give up even a fraction of their material well-being to ease someone else's misery. Moreover, just as many people believed that the South Vietnamese themselves should have won the war, they also believe that poverty does and should persist. If the poor, they insist, would only work and save and stop having so many children, they could make it like everyone else. But the problem of poverty, like that of the war, is hard not only because it involves conflicts between rich and poor or Communist and non-Communist, but because proposed solutions reveal conflicts in the outcomes sought by *both* the rich and the poor, the Communist and the non-Communist.

Consider, for example, the almost total agreement about the necessity for welfare reform and the widespread disagreement about how to accomplish it. Part of this disagreement may be due to the nonpoor's unwillingness to give aid to the poor, but more of it is due to the extreme difficulty of simultaneously resolving several conflicting outcomes. This differs in no substantial way from the problems encountered during the Vietnam War. The complexity of reconciling conflicting outcomes can perhaps best be seen by placing some of the goals of welfare and war side by side:

A welfare system should assure everyone at least a minimum adequate level of income. A war's outcome should assure everyone at least a minimum adequate level of personal and political freedom.

A welfare system ought to encourage people to work. A war ought to be fought to preserve and defend institutions and values esteemed by a nation's citizens.

A welfare system should be fair, to the extent that equally disadvantaged people should receive equal treatment, no matter who they are or where they live. A war's burden should be shared to the extent that no class or group is required to make excessive personal sacrifices or is able to profit from the war at the expense of another group.

It is obvious that both our present welfare system and the Vietnam War produced outcomes in conflict with those legitimate objectives. Couldn't we have done better? I think not—not because the problems of welfare and war are beyond solution, but rather because finding a solution that satisfactorily avoids conflicting outcomes is not easy. For too long, in both these areas, we were led to believe that the spending of federal money and the massive commitment of military resources would help, but we were either conditioned or willing to accept out of laziness that it was not necessary to worry about the outcomes of our actions. This was a fatal error. The design problems are extremely hard to solve and even harder to explain to those who must live with the outcomes.

If we are to overcome the consequences of failure and resolve the stresses of pollution, resource demands, and food requirements in America and elsewhere, it is absolutely essential that we approach the complex of environmental problems with will power, intelligence, and compassion. The pollution problem is perhaps the most significant, because it is one about which the American public may feel it is worth paying the necessary costs to stop fouling its nest. The pollution of our environment at home and the destruction of Vietnamese society are uncomfortably similar. Both were the product of the highest of motives, in that pollution was the natural by-product of the United States becoming the strongest, most affluent, most technologically advanced nation in the world and Vietnam was destroyed in an effort to "save" it, and both have resulted in a situation where the persons who were the ostensible objects of altruism have suffered while those responsible were largely unaffected.

Long before pollution became an issue of national concern I knew something was wrong. As a boy I didn't need Barry Commoner to tell me about the "closing circle." Living near the Union Stockyards in Chicago, I needed only to breathe, smell, and look at the decay surrounding those living in what today is called the inner-city ghetto. Pollution, like hand-to-hand combat and carpet bombing, it not an abstraction. It is a real hazard to the urban poor. The threat of ecological genocide is about to be faced at a time when the death throes are already being felt in America's inner cities. The environmentalists are probably too late; they have stayed too long in the wilderness. Vietnam is no different. The uneasy peace that came in 1973 was too long overdue. But we must at least make an effort.

These, then, are the parameters to the consequences of our military failure: a social and institutional structure in serious disarray; a lack of confidence in our leaders; an unwillingness to face the sacrifices we must make to solve our nearly overwhelming domestic problems; and a condition of environmental disequilibrium that affects the quality of daily life in a thousand ways, ranging from mindless violence to class conflicts and widespread dissatisfaction with America's cultural and ethical value systems. Young people are asking for a cause. The cause is here. It is to overcome failure. It will be a very difficult battle to fight. Yet we should be less than those who have preceded us in man's search for freedom and dignity if we didn't try. We live in our time. This is the responsibility and the heritage of our failure in Vietnam.

NINE

To Overcome Failure

"You cannot do the things that need to be done, as I call it to wage the peace, merely with arms. You have got to have human understanding of human wants, and you have got to make it possible to achieve something in satisfying those wants if we are going to wage peace successfully."

—Dwight D. Eisenhower

THE CONSEQUENCES of military failure in Vietnam, both indirect and direct, have yet to be fully felt. We have reacted very much like someone with all the warning signals of cancer who refuses to see a doctor for fear that what he already feels and knows about his condition will be confirmed. Successive national administrations have redefined the aims of our extended participation in the war in an attempt to avoid a public reckoning about it. By any objective standards none of the various goals was achieved. To claim, for example, that we have peace with honor because when we withdrew our troops from Vietnam we got our POWs back does not make it true and does not change the fact of our failure. It only delays consideration of its consequences.

Thus the necessary first step to overcome failure is to at least acknowledge the fact that we *have* failed. It will be painful, but only if we confuse acknowledgment of the fact with the need to blame someone for it. There is sufficient blame to go around so that we can all have as much or as little as we need to salve our individual consciences. There is no way to make our decade of military involvement in Vietnam a "nonevent" by laying it on the

doorsteps of McNamara, Rostow, McGeorge Bundy, Westmoreland, *et al.* True, they bear a large measure of responsibility for
U.S. Vietnam policy, but to blame them is to ascribe a baseness
to their motives that never existed; they discharged their responsibilities according to their own lights.

If we are talking about blame in the sense of knowing something was wrong and remaining silent or deferring to authority
for authority's sake, it lies in the actions of thousands of persons
like myself who failed to communicate effectively what we knew
and believed to those in charge. This blame and the personal guilt
it implies I fully accept, but in no way does this obviate the
need to act to overcome the consequences of failure. We must de-
personalize the issue. Quite literally, we can lose our way as a
nation of free men and women if we engage in recriminations
against those who for one reason or another too persistently pursued the impossible dream of military victory in the no-win environment of an ideological war.

Uncertainty seems to dominate our approach to the consequences of military failure in Vietnam. Uncertainty with an edge
of fear? Perhaps. It is a dangerous condition that can quickly de-
generate into a paralyzing and destructive one. The Vietnam War
and its traumatizing effects are the source of our current difficulties, but—as we have shown—we are not the first people in
history to have this kind of experience or to be required to seek
an answer to the question of how to overcome failure. It does
seem—and though the feeling is subjective on my part, it is
strong and I have heard it consistently expressed by the young,
the old, the great and the near-great, and those whose lives and
futures were dependent upon the continued successful performance of America's institutions—that our nation had gone past
its point of no return. It is an eerie condition that gives the impression of a people waiting for a malevolent god or a combination of circumstances to punish them for their past transgressions.
This is not particularly strange. We can't enjoy our isolation and
moral neutrality as unself-consciously as once we did because we
are haunted by My Lai and the shadow of all those bomb clouds
over all of Vietnam.

Our problem in overcoming failure is not based on a shortage of data—we know a tremendous amount about what went on in Vietnam, what is going on in other countries, and what is going on in our own country—but on our inability to see the consequences of the information we already possess, particularly the immediate prospect of the breakdown of our institutional system. We know it is happening. We see it in the alienation of the young, the rejection of time-tested values, and the widespread indifference to our individual responsibility to participate in the search for solutions to the problems that threaten to destroy the world society in which we all must live. The ancient philosophers teach that despair is a sin because it prevents a man from trying to right a wrong, create a good, or overcome failure. No matter how small the action, it must be attempted without waiting for disaster to strike or for all the data to become available. This, then, is the second step to overcome failure.

Not that we should not rely on measurable data when we can, but we should also be willing to rely on intuition, insight, and hunches. For example, there came a time in Vietnam when I noticed that the people who had been moved from their homes by our government were no longer responding to each other's needs, and it occurred to me that some of the stoic and phlegmatic members of the group were becoming increasingly hostile toward our efforts to assist them. I acted upon those general observations as true ones without waiting for statistical confirmation in the form of rocket attacks and ambushes aided by those who had become alienated because of our actions.

In "pure" science the practice is "I see it but it's meaningless, so we'll ignore it until we get all the data"—a practice, I might add, not unlike that used by our government in dealing with problems. The implied issue here, as I see it, is the necessity to find out a great deal about reality and simultaneously study the total interaction. If we only deal with small pieces of reality based upon the hope that someday, somehow, they can be put back together we will lose sight of the real world they presently constitute. Normal, or "applied," science, which eliminates variables and examines situations piece by piece, is inadequate because life is not that way, and if we simplify life to that degree we most certainly will lose life. If we are to survive, let alone overcome failure, we cannot adopt either the pure or the applied approach exclusively. We must act now on the basis of less than full information and be prepared to shift our emphasis and direction quickly. To do otherwise is to invite disaster, in both the long and short run.

I don't mean anything at all subtle. It goes almost without saying that to reverse the breakdown of our institutional system there has to be major commitment to change. It also goes without saying that to overcome failure and avoid future catastrophes at home and abroad there has to be something more than uneasy understanding about the failure in Vietnam, something more positive than indifference to our situation.

But what is that something? Perhaps it is the kind of cooperation that many persons have been trying to promote among nations and peoples. Perhaps it is agreement that there must be more than "peaceful coexistence" between the two great power centers of the world if we are to avoid a food and population disaster in the so-called Third World in the next twenty years. Although none of this is likely to happen, we should still act to repair the damage to our institutions as an essential step in order to keep our country safe, because if we don't, there is no way for us to prevent suffering and desperation in many countries on a scale as yet unknown, and our apparent tendency to regress and turn inward, away from our and others' problems, will continue to grow.

This may be the ultimate consequence of our failure in Vietnam, and—if we have any concern about our nation and the world in which we must all live—it is the last thing we want to happen. We badly need an unafraid, bold, thoughtful, purposeful America to speak to the world's problems of war and peace. Unless we repair the damage done to our institutions and environment in the past decade—which will require much greater sacrifice on the part of ordinary citizens than the United States has

ever exacted in any war—our country will not be able to play
that role. And that is the third step we must take in overcoming
failure.

It doesn't seem that such sacrifices will happen voluntarily.
We are all selfish, and to stint ourselves to pay off the cost of the
Vietnam War, or to avoid future institutional and ecological
disasters, just doesn't appear to be in the cards. Too many persons are convinced that our present affluence and power can be
maintained without paying the Vietnam fiddler. Maybe so, but
the history of other nations after a failure in a political-ideo-
logical war suggests otherwise.

To give the issue some added perspective, I am going to give
three different possible outcomes during President Nixon's "generation of peace." Each is a projection based upon our current
reactions, the situation to date in our institutional structure, and
the actions taken by our formal and informal leadership in response to the fact of our military failure in Vietnam.

Outcome Number One is the gloomiest and, I am afraid, the
most likely.

The relations between the United States and the major powers will not change much, except that we will become more dependent on the Soviet Union and they upon us for the exchange
of raw materials, especially natural gas and other petroleum products for American foodstuffs and grains. Also, the likelihood of
nuclear war between the superpowers will recede, but the pro-
liferation of nuclear weapons will continue. One can visualize
minor but extremely dangerous wars in which nuclear weapons
may be used, but even that would not produce a major nuclear
exchange between the superpowers. We and our Russian and
Chinese "allies" will agree to let others disagree, even to the extent of allowing Jerusalem to become nuclearized without launching our own weapons in retaliation. The minimum amount of coexistence will be preserved.

Our relations with the European Common Market nations
will continue to worsen because of our monetary and trade policies. Our attempts to export America's inflation will meet with

even less success than our efforts to export our form of democracy
to South Vietnam. The Italians, Japanese, and Germans will return our inflation to us in spades redoubled, causing Congress to
rise up in righteous indignation and pass protectionist trade measures. This will add to our domestic turmoil as prices continue
to rise, but it will give us a sense of unity: a hatred of Europeans,
who will become the *bête noire* of our domestic difficulties.
Politics will lead economics, and, in spite of incipient inflation,
both the American and Soviet societies will get richer. The rest of
the technologically developed nations will polarize toward either
the United States, the Soviet Union, or China, and a new uneasy
balance of power between the "advanced" nations and the "have
not" nations will emerge. It promises to be a period in which the
great and near-great powers will practice "benign neglect" toward those nations living at or below subsistence level.

We will see it all. Millions of people are going to starve to
death, in living color on the evening news, and Walter Cronkite
will tell us that's the way it is. Famine will become commonplace.
It may become, before the end of the "generation of peace,"
endemic to all but the most technologically advanced countries
who have the guns to fight off the hungry millions outside their
borders. We have been psychologically prepared by Vietnam to
be indifferent to suffering outside our borders; the horror of starv-
ing millions is not so different from the horror of the "antiseptic"
bombing of North and South Vietnam.

All of this is likely to lead to even greater isolationism because, as a people, we have been thoroughly indoctrinated to believe that in the collision between rising population and available
food supplies the experts can pull something out of their collective hats to keep us safe and comfortable. It may well be a period
in which forays into Asia, Africa, and Latin America to acquire
raw materials to keep our industrial technological world turning
will be as ruthless as were those to acquire slaves in the early
nineteenth century. How long would *you* be willing to let the
sheiks of the Middle East sit on their oil reserves in the face of
gas rationing, "heatless weekends," and widespread brownouts in
the United States? The "liberation" of Middle Eastern oil might

then seem justified and in accord with the natural order of a Darwinian world.

Domestically, the situation will be much the same. Deterioration of national commitments will continue in such apparently disparate areas as equal-hearing standards in the power industry and federal-contract compliance as well as in the more visible ones like equal educational and job opportunity. Social relations will regress as we turn inward, away from the sticky problem of learning how to live together. Many social-welfare and environmental needs will be by-passed because the cost will be adjudged excessive by those with the political and economic power to vote them down. There will be lower and lower voter turnout in almost all elections except local ones where the "hot button" issue of the moment coincides with election day. Issues will become more and more transitory; the problem of today that can't be solved tomorrow will be forgotten. It may come to be known as the era of the "credibility crisis," when the difference between the fact and promise in most areas of human endeavor will be highlighted and emphasized to the point that confidence in ourselves and our institutions will be shattered. Modern-day muckrakers will have a field day, at least for a short time, as the strident sound of rip-offs drowns out the sounds of those who may still continue to strive to repair and improve the system and make it work.

This negativism may breed its own form of counterreaction whereby the power structure will feel so imperiled that it will act to gain complete control over the dissident elements in the system. These are uneasy times and the right of any individual or group to oppose the "social good" or necessity is suspect. It matters not who is in the White House; the power structure cannot tolerate active indifference to its laws and edicts. In this sense, indifference is a less active form of opposition than an overt revolt or uprising, but in a modern state that is almost totally dependent upon the continued acceptance of its regulations, it can be more devastating. Our final innocence was lost in Vietnam, and from here on it is likely that those who stand in the way of action deemed necessary for our national security or "advancement" will be ground up like leaves in a backyard shredder.

The America we are describing differs substantially from the one portrayed on our TV sets, but only by degrees from the one that has already come into being as a result of the physical requirements to maintain our scale of living. The ultimate choice is between a major curtailment of our living standards for the next twenty years and the sheer taking of what we require from the rest of the world, especially the so-called underdeveloped countries. Today, propriety and morality is less a concern because, as a nation, we have become inured to the criticism of other nations and of dissident elements in our own population about our Vietnam policies, for which no rational explanation can be given.

Outcome Number Two is somewhat less draconian. It is likely to occur if the acrimony surrounding the consequences of our military failure is replaced quickly by the sense of isolation and turning inward that began to gain momentum in the last year of the war.

As in the first scenario, there will be a successful avoidance of nuclear war between the superpowers and a scaling down of military spending on the part of both the United States and the Soviet Union, but neither country will use any funds saved on military expenditures to provide food, money, or technical assistance to the poor nations. The harsh realities of the budget squeeze, the conflict between the environment and the energy shortage, and growing resistance within American industry to economic restraints strongly mitigate against the diversion of any significant amount of funds to anyone else.

What we are talking about is the creation of a "Fortress America" in which the leaders and population will not be willing to make any sacrifices to aid the rest of the world but might—provided the leadership of the country were sufficiently decisive, persuasive, and constructive—be willing to tighten its belt enough to deal with its own domestic problems. There would not be the "economic imperialism" of raiding other countries for their natural resources, characteristic of Outcome Number One, but hard-nosed "cash and carry" attempts to get what is needed through no-nonsense trade agreements. In a sense, the United States would be in a state of siege as far as her relations with the rest of the world went.

Realistically speaking, there is some merit in this scenario, because there is scant assurance that anything we might choose to do could head off disaster in the poor countries of the world anyway. In fact, any action we might unilaterally take to aid them would be at least equally likely to make conditions worse for them. This harsh reality provides adequate rationalization for a national policy of indifference toward the underdeveloped countries and fits in well with the valid notion that a strong America is to be absolutely preferred to a weak one.

Under this outcome the public will probably still regard economic growth as a proper national objective, but might see the necessity of efforts to bring it into reasonable harmony with other domestic goals such as protection of the natural environment, safety from crime and disorder, fair distribution of personal income, stable prices, decentralization of government, personal freedom, and a renewal of moral discipline. Relating these goals to each other is no mean task, but in one form or another they form part of what most Americans now want from their society and what they may be prepared to support as a post-Vietnam national policy.

Some politicians will contend that we lack the option of withdrawing into a position of passive political isolation, but the cold wind of voter opposition to the use of tax dollars for other than America's domestic needs will quickly silence them. Economic assistance for North and South Vietnam is bound sooner or later to become the rallying point in the quest for a restrictive foreign policy. Even if this foreign policy results in a series of sporadic and violent responses leading to minor wars such as those between India and Pakistan—in which, in the future, nuclear weapons might be used—it does not seem likely that the United States would become involved, either before or after the fact. The belief that America can prevent or influence the outcome of conflicts between other nations—until recently an article of faith with liberals and conservatives alike—has been shattered by the realization, born of the Vietnam War, that there are physical and ideological limits to the amount of support the American people are willing to give other nations' people or politicians.

Outcome Number Three is by far the most unlikely of the three, yet if the worldwide chaos that is both implicit and explicit in the other two alternatives is not to occur we have to act as though it is more likely than it is. There are some in our nation who still believe that the only decent response to the consequences of our military failure in Vietnam is to act to overcome them domestically and yet continue to fulfill our obligations to provide world leadership, or at least try to. Most of the time, a nation's citizens are concerned only with their own welfare. But although we have to take selfishness pretty much for granted, we can also rely on human intelligence. For all of America's faults, and there are many, our basic intelligence has been the strength of our nation in times of adversity. It is perhaps our best and only hope now if we are to overcome our failure in Vietnam.

In Outcome Number Three we must know the facts; we must have what President Nixon promised in 1969—"an open government." The American people must understand the ominous implications of the two preceding scenarios and know the economic and social costs of any policies we may inaugurate. It is going to call for great sacrifices, especially on the part of those who have had it so good for so long. If we are to overcome failure, we are going to have to go out into the streets in which that failure is a constant, nagging reminder of the difference between rhetoric and reality.

This outcome differs from the others because it meets the real dangers our nation is facing. It is a very difficult course of action because it requires a long-term commitment to an uncertain outcome. It transcends everything we have come to understand by the term "foreign aid" because it will mean using political and economic resources for distant ends that are ideological only in the sense that peace, food, and no more people than the earth can take is ideological. The really hard part of this approach is that since we alone could never avert the disaster looming ahead for the world's poor countries, there will have to be a truly cooperative, concerted effort by the United States, Western Europe, the Soviet Union, and Japan to bring about a sustained balance of worldwide resource utilization, food production, and population. Frankly, it is difficult to believe that this will happen or that it will even be actively considered in the current political climate and at a time when the pressures for domestic reform and rehabilitation inveigh against looking beyond our borders for additional problems.

These three possible outcomes are not exhaustive, but they do contain the elements of the choices and dilemmas posed by the consequences of our military failure in Vietnam. No choice is going to be easy. As we have shown, the consequences of failure have been manifested in a series of personal and institutional shock waves that have already resulted in regressive actions in many areas of personal and institutional behavior. As a people, we have become extremely hesitant to try new ways to solve the problems revealed and caused by Vietnam. And because the comfortable and familiar ways have produced such disastrous results, we seem content to tread water in the hope that somehow the consequences of failure will just go away.

Thinking about the unthinkable has never been our long suit. In our past history there has always been some combination of fortuitous circumstances that came to the rescue, but the Vietnam aftermath bids fair to be far different. There are no easy solutions for the problems we have raised, just hard choices among harsh alternatives. Yet the fact that the global issues and alternatives are not fully developed, and the fact that the problems are incredibly complex, does not absolve any of us from trying to see the total situation because only in that way may we begin to change it.

In concluding this chapter, I would like to make one specific suggestion about overcoming failure and one very special plea. The former concerns a method of "repairing" one of our major institutions, the latter our Vietnam veterans.

How does one go about repairing institutions? The best way I can think of is to try to rejuvenate and reform them, and to modify their performance so that they are able to do what they were originally supposed to do and perhaps something more. I'd like to suggest, as an example, what might be done to repair some of the damage done to the military establishment by means of a military domestic action program.

Although I am limiting my proposal to the military, the methodology has general applications for other institutions. It provides a logical, practical way of evaluating possible actions that may be useful in overcoming failure in other areas by developing a new conceptual scheme, and provides the fundamental principles to understand a problem and so develop genuine expertise in any similar area. It is only a beginning, an alternative approach to despair. But until those who manage society's institutions can be convinced it is worth while to act, and to act in new and different ways, there is little chance for success. I suggest that the reader think of how this methodology can be applied in other areas, and ask "Why not?"

As we noted in an earlier chapter, these are not happy times for America's military establishment. Wars are unfashionable. There have been serious racial and drug-abuse problems in each of the services, anti-war dissent in the ranks, a weakening of the chain of command, and, finally, a serious questioning within the officer corps of the premises and values on which its professional life is based—the concepts of duty, honor, and country. "Today," Brigadier General Theodore Mataxis wrote in the January 1971 issue of *The Army* magazine, "the services are facing the signs of disruption of discipline which could lead to anarchy and defeat on the battlefield." The Department of Defense, however, in its Statement of Human Goals, has chosen to re-emphasize the role of the military in our society through domestic action, in the following words: "to contribute to the improvement of our society, including its disadvantaged members, by greater utilization of our human and physical resources while maintaining full effectiveness in the performance of our primary mission." *

Historically, the military services have played a significant

* *Commanders Digest,* November 1, 1969.

but largely unpublicized role in implementing domestic policies and improving U.S. society. In addition to fighting the Indian wars, the Army played a valuable role in opening the frontier by helping local communities plan and harvest their crops and managing three out of the four western railroads built by 1900. Military medical efforts provide an even more impressive testimonial to the constructive potential of the armed services; in 1900 there were three hundred fifty thousand cases of typhoid fever in the United States, and an Army Medical Board team headed by Major Walter Reed eliminated this health problem. Other Army medical teams developed methods for controlling yellow fever, beriberi, and malaria.

The economic development of the United States was promoted by the work of the Army's Corps of Engineers, which, in addition to its well-publicized flood and disaster relief work, has completed thirty-six hundred major engineering or construction projects, built or improved more than three hundred harbors, and constructed and maintained more than thirty thousand miles of coastal and inland waterways.

The military's ability to carry out domestic action projects was also seen in the Army's role in the Civilian Conservation Corps (CCC), one of the New Deal "workfare" programs organized in 1933 to provide employment in the field of conservation for single men between the ages of eighteen and twenty-five. Initially, responsibility for the CCC was to be shared by the Departments of Interior and Agriculture, but it soon became obvious that these departments were incapable of running the program. As a result, the Chief Forester requested the Army take over the major responsibility for administering and setting up the CCC. The request was honored, and the results speak for themselves: within eighty days after the Army took over, thirteen hundred conservation camps were in operation, staffed by both Regular and Reserve officers. In less than eight years three and a half million young men had participated successfully in the program and many million acres of denuded land had been reforested.

Nonetheless, the case supporting the use of America's

military forces in a domestic/civic action role to help solve current social problems remains essentially unproven. There are those, both in and out of the military, who argue that efforts spent on domestic action programs would detract from military preparedness, certainly a valid consideration. Yet in certain situations, military commitments can be restructured in such a way that they are matched against social and domestic action priorities without any diminution in a unit's combat readiness, and in fact might even enhance it. For example, aiding local authorities initiate and carry out a drug-abuse education and treatment program might help commanders at all levels understand more about the drug problem in their own units.

There are those, on the other hand, who argue that the morale of every serviceman would be improved as a result of participating in domestic action projects, making it easier for him to pursue his military requirements with greater interest. There is some evidence to support this view, but it is essential that only the best-trained and most highly motivated men are used to carry out domestic action projects, and that it not be used primarily as a morale-booster.

Project Nation Building, which began in January 1971, is a good case in point. It was an experiment, essentially a pilot project, conceived by Lieutenant General John J. Tolson to use the civic action skills of Special Forces teams in two extremely poor North Carolina counties—Hoke and Anson—adjacent to Fort Bragg. Special Forces teams worked at a variety of different tasks—clearing out clogged drainage ditches, repairing public buildings, teaching physical fitness in local schools—and medics in each of the teams assisted the Public Health nurses in taking and reading blood tests, immunizations, urinalyses, and paperwork. Dr. Riley Jordan, one of Hoke County's two private physicians, said of the Special Forces, "They are serving a tremendous local need. A lot of people are being seen who wouldn't otherwise be seen." *

Clearly, the efforts of the Special Forces in Hoke and Anson counties, and in Glenn Springs, South Carolina, and at Lame

---

* "Nation Mending at Home," *Time*, June 21, 1971.

Deer on the Tongue River Indian Reservation in Montana, demonstrated their capacity to carry out military domestic action projects. However, these were very select units, and their excellent record does not guarantee that similar results could be achieved by other Army units, let alone the other military services. At the present time, Department of Defense opinion is divided over whether the experimental efforts of the Special Forces should be expanded to a nationwide program with participation by each of the military services.

A basic consideration is that the military does not initiate or conduct domestic action on its own; it only supports local activities. Can the military design a methodology for solving problems that could be effectively transferred to the local environment, and can the local authorities be encouraged to understand and implement the design effectively and efficiently? The often overlooked gap between conceiving a program and then having someone else carry it out is critical to the ultimate effectiveness of military domestic action. This is probably the greatest single handicap to the military in developing an expanded domestic action program: determining what is really relevant and what really can be made to work.

Another consideration should be noted. Political exigencies, both at the national and local level, are likely to be the primary determinants of the overall military domestic action role, and any politicization of the military is not without hazard. America's military men and the people they help cannot and must not be allowed to become any group's political guinea pig or stalking horse. Quite obviously, pressures are bound to mount to use the sheer power, size, and capacity of the military for more than nonproductive, repetitive training and flag showing. Restructuring the military so that it can help cure social ills while maintaining combat readiness is currently feasible in many cases.

For example, without interfering in the activities of committed active contingent units, a Naval Reserve Construction Battalion (Seabees) of approximately a thousand men could spend its annual two weeks of active duty constructing and refurbishing schools, hospitals, and living quarters on an Indian reservation, or a Reserve Army Field Hospital Unit could be ordered to a hard-core poverty area in Appalachia to provide medical and dental assistance. The point is, of course, that not only can this be done by the military, and done exceedingly well, but it is the kind of thing likely to remain undone if left strictly to other federal and local government agencies. While no one will deny the merit of these kinds of activities, they are far from being apolitical in nature because of the implication that the normal channels are not capable of carrying them out on their own. There is a political side to domestic action, and it must be dealt with realistically if disruptive counterproductive results are to be avoided.

In the light of the vast array of social problems confronting us, it is inappropriate to speak of "a" military role. Rather, we must think in terms of many federal government domestic action roles and of how the military can best be utilized in carrying out specific projects as necessary. If military domestic action is adopted as a national policy, the individual military commander will be required to do the best possible job in any particular situation. It is important, therefore, that before undertaking any program he measures it against criteria that will help him ascertain its relevance and potential effectiveness in solving a specific problem in a specific local community.

This "preassessment" should take into consideration the cause and nature of the problem; the policy objectives by which the program will be judged; what support will be available, both from the federal government and the local community; the nature of the local environment and its people, and particularly of the social and political climate; the strategy of the local opposition, if any; how the local government operates and how it sees the problem; Department of Defense and/or national political considerations; the extent to which the Department of Defense and the national administration are interested in the particular situation, and the funds and resources they can be expected to make available.

In some rare cases a program might be carried out even if the result of the preassessment indicated that there would be little chance for complete success of the program or for complete cooperation with local authorities, if *not* to take action would mean that the local conditions would deteriorate to such an extent as to be potentially explosive. In other words, in some cases, a decision to do nothing would in fact mean doing something in a negative sense, and this kind of situation should be avoided if possible. Obviously, a program carried out in such circumstances would have to be even more carefully planned than when the preassessment indicated the situation was more conducive to domestic military participation.

Once the preassessment is made and the military commander has a realistic grasp of the situation, actually rendering the assistance is primarily a matter of skillfully using appropriate military resources and expertise within the framework of the local government's approach to the social problem. In this connection, it is important to remember that the military has certain capacities that make it potentially very effective in carrying out domestic action programs. They are: advisory, operational, supportive, and instructional personnel; equipment, installations, raw materials, food; appropriated and nonappropriated funds; the ability to train local government officials in military facilities or in the local environment; the technical expertise to analyze and evaluate on-going program performance.

Care must be taken to recognize that military domestic action is not a formula process. For such a program to have a reasonable chance for success, the problem under attack must be continually reassessed, and the methods used must be flexible enough to keep abreast of changing conditions as well as emerging new problems. The planning and evaluation criteria are applicable at any time, but a set of basic principles on which a sound program can be built will round out the picture.

These guidelines are important not only for the military commander but for the local authorities, because the interaction between the military and the local political infrastructure is fraught with danger for both if domestic action is looked upon by either one or the other as a gimmick to "pacify" the population rather than as a positive, genuine, joint effort to achieve a constructive goal. Just as the military's outlook and approach must be adapted to a particular domestic problem, so must the local political apparatus be flexible in its attitude toward partnership with the military. There are many pitfalls inherent in the military/local government interaction process, and these guidelines are offered to point out how some of them may be avoided. Although the listings are fairly comprehensive, they should be considered neither exhaustive nor an attempt to cast a unified field theory for military intervention in domestic social conflict.

Guidelines for Local Government Officials

1. Have a definable political objective that is attuned to the traditional value systems of the population.

2. Establish an organizational mechanism for maintaining the focus on the problem selected for action and for planning specific local and military strategy that balances all the area's interests.

3. Assess carefully the causes and nature of the problem and other key elements in order to determine whether or not military assistance will be helpful in resolving it.

4. Since the causes of social problems are fluid, once the program is in operation it must be constantly assessed to determine whether it should be adjusted in any way.

5. Set up an effective communication channel with the people of the community directly affected by the problem to make sure that the real priorities are in the forefront.

6. The local government should maintain its own organization and managerial integrity so that the program will not collapse once the military participation ends.

7. Approach the problem through either the causal route (social change) or the resource route (mobilization-stabilization). Since inequities and lack of appropriate resources are the two basic elements of any social problem, if the government does not utilize one of these methods it will merely deal with the effects of a problem rather than the underlying causes.

8. Recognize that the separate strategic areas of national

policy (regional redevelopment, successive "wars" on poverty, federal manpower-training programs, etc.) represent an attempt to achieve broad social change and realignments of power, wealth, and opportunity and that within these areas a range of options or compromise possibilities exist that can be used to help address social problems and their causes in local areas.

9. Structure strategies in such a way that they contribute to overall national efforts or policy, thereby possibly qualifying for federal assistance that might not otherwise be available to the program.

10. Organize a public-education effort that combines domestic action objectives with those of private, fraternal, and social organizations in order to elicit the widest possible support.

Guidelines for Military Personnel

1. Assess the social problems in the specific area to determine their precise nature, in accord with overall national policy. Include an examination of the possible tools that can be provided and their suitability in the local environment.

2. Plan strategy in such a way that it helps the local organization to enlist the support of the local government as well as supplement performance requirements.

3. The program should be divorced as much as possible from identification with local political parties, and should contribute to the long-term interests of the local population.

4. The enactment of the program should not stand in the way of natural forces that can bring about needed social-political changes in the local environment. This is a difficult principle; by its very nature, the participation of the military is likely to inhibit—at least temporarily—those persons seeking social change who are outside the existing power structure.

5. Efforts should be geared to allow the development of local institutions that are responsive to the particular needs and values of the people, and not be prescribed in the abstract from the national level.

6. A central coordinator should plan the contributions of each military service in a unified effort.

7. In the local environment, the policy of the national co-ordinator should be consistently implemented by individual military commanders and their organizations.

8. The program should not be so sophisticated that the local government cannot maintain it on its own in the future.

9. The military activities should generally be supportive in nature, except in those rare cases when the President determines that a social problem (not a natural disaster or a riot) directly threatens the national interest and therefore directs the military to assume an active operational role.

10. Recognize the inherent limitations of some military tools for domestic action purposes and work to make them more adaptive.

Turning from a consideration of the military establishment to the men who serve in it, I would suggest that an extremely important step in overcoming failure should be to acknowledge and pay our debts to those who executed our national policy in the rice paddies and jungles of Vietnam, Laos, and Cambodia. These are the men for whom there were no victory parades, no accolades, no special bonuses, benefits, or gifts; they were the poor bastards who day in, day out, put their lives and limbs on the line to carry out our national quest for "peace with honor." There is no way to equate their sacrifices with those of men who suffered the unimaginable agonies of up to eight years of imprisonment, or of the more than half a million ex-GIs who lost limbs or were seriously disabled in the war. Nor is there a need to. We owe the former POWs something special, but not to the exclusion of something equally special for those who slugged it out on the ground with the Viet Cong one night and the curse of heroin the next and got back to the United States in what appears on the surface to be one piece.

The POWs were, for the most part, highly trained mature officers. Undoubtedly they will carry some scars that will never quite heal, but at least they came home with a feeling of pride that somehow the years torn out of their lives were worth it. They also came home to the first positive shared emotion about Vietnam that the American people felt throughout the war's dreary course. They were comfortable heroes for all Americans, but especially for President Nixon, because they voiced support for his war policies, because they were trim and cheerful, and because their good condition was apparently due in large measure to their ability to maintain military discipline and a firm chain of command while they were in captivity.

Theirs was a captivity without precedent in any of America's wars. There is no way to compare the treatment meted out to the residents of the "Hanoi Hilton" with that to, say, those at Andersonville. They were not forced to labor in their own behalf, nor were they isolated from one another. The issue of their torture is irrelevant, or at least moot, in view of the question about "how much" torture you should sustain before "confessing." They were, in fact, treated as criminals doing time under an indefinite sentence rather than as true POWs. Part of this was due to the North Vietnamese, who used them as a trump ace in the long truce negotiations and who became convinced early in the war that those pilots unlucky enough to wind up under their control would cause their jailers no trouble. The camps in North Vietnam were particularly well organized. All prisoners participated in a rigorous exercise program, one explanation for their general good health. But there were no escape committees and there were no organized attempts to continue the fight. Theirs was a period of captivity that can only be described as a kind of suspended animation in which they did what was necessary to survive, maintain their sanity and physical well-being, and not much more. Their war ended the moment they were taken into custody. Their choice not to continue to oppose the enemy will be debated for years in the war colleges, but it, like most elements of the war, will quickly become a minor footnote to the history of our involvement in Vietnam.

By an almost incredible coincidence, in February 1973 when the POWs were returning, the Nixon administration surfaced a plan to reduce benefits for veterans who were seriously disabled in the Vietnam War. The timing could not have been more disastrous, but the wounded veterans had powerful friends in Congress who quickly came to their assistance, and the proposed changes were promptly withdrawn. Like the POWs, the crippled veterans are a special case, and both have their defenders who can be counted on to make sure that the "cost-effective" non-combatants in the Office of Management and Budget are not able to practice their perverse economies at the expense of either group. But those ex-GIs who are not considered "special" are not likely to fare as well.

The Vietnam veteran who somehow made it through the long nights of violence and fear has been all but forgotten by the American government and its people. They came back as they went to Vietnam—one by one, alone with their memories, hates, and hostilities. In the February 1973 issue of *Human Behavior,* Dr. Chaim F. Shatan tried to tell us what the Vietnam veteran felt: "The shame and guilt of being alive. How few of us know what that feels like, how it makes a man feel less than whole unless he can identify with the dead. The Veterans Administration does not know, because it has refused to recognize the unique experience of the 'grunts.' Today's veteran returns unheralded and unwanted to an ambivalent nation. Due to the rotation system, they come back piecemeal, one at a time, without their units, without their buddies, without their usual victory parades. They return to an administration which does little to tend to their wounds, less to continue their education and even less to find them work." William Raspberry, writing in the *Washington Post* on February 16, 1973, also tried to warn us: "The Vietnam veteran, having been called upon to participate in a war that was both a military and domestic disaster, then coming home to a nation that is largely ungrateful, and on top of it finding it next to impossible to find decent work, does represent something of a *time bomb.*"

We all know this, but prefer not to think about it. Tens of thousands of Vietnam veterans are jobless and growing more bitter toward their country and the "establishment" every day. They are back in the ghettos from which they went to Vietnam and in which unemployment is not merely a monthly statistic announced by the Bureau of Labor Statistics, but a pervasive fact of their daily lives. These are the young men who were the cutting edge on our "incursion" into Cambodia and who now curse when they see how much easier it is to get a cease-fire in the war on poverty than it was to find the elusive COSVN head-quarters in Cambodia. These are the young men who are becoming increasingly angered by talk of dismantling the social programs on which they and their families depend so that money will be available for the rehabilitation and rebuilding of North and South Vietnam.

These veterans deserve something better from all of us. They are our national responsibility, and if more taxes are required to provide them with adequate health, job, and education benefits, the taxes should be levied and earmarked for this specific purpose, as was done in the case of the interstate highway system. We cannot afford *not* to make sure the Vietnam veteran is provided with what he needs to become a full-time member of American society.

In addition to simple economic equity, there are two other major reasons for unstinting support of the Vietnam veteran. One is the necessity to defuse his potential for violence against those he sees as the cause of his current problems. The other is the necessity to rectify the inherent inequality of the way we got the men we needed to fight the war.

Whether we like it or not, most Vietnam veterans have had it with all parts of the "establishment," and if a major effort isn't made to "unprogram" these young men from attempting to solve their problems by pulling a trigger we are going to find that many of them will be doing a lot of stateside killing. We trained them to solve their personal problems of survival in Vietnam's hostile environment by shooting first and asking questions later; there is no reason to assume that they will not resort to a similar solution in America's hostile environment. We must make a more determined effort to train them to solve their personal, social, and economic problems in a constructive way. Each day we delay we increase the probability that the Vietnam veteran's alienation from society will become irreversible and total. This is a consequence of our military failure that we can and must act to overcome. We owe it to the Vietnam veterans and to the forty-six thousand families whose young men made a bigger sacrifice than even the most bedraggled POW.

The second reason has ugly implications that extend beyond our immediate concern for the Vietnam veterans into the very moral fabric of our society. The procedures by which we met the manpower needs to fight the Vietnam war were highly discriminatory; the cards were stacked against the children from blue-collar families and from the black, brown, and red ghettos. No equality of sacrifice was either planned or intended by our lawmakers. The children of the affluent who were able to stay in college or escape into subsidized early marriages were almost totally exempt from military service. Nor did those young men who were permitted to continue their draft-deferred education volunteer to serve as commissioned officers upon their graduation; they clogged America's graduate schools in order to avoid military service of any sort. They were not the protesters or conscientious objectors, who in most cases were acting on the basis of some kind of moral conviction or belief. Many of these young men, in fact, vocally supported President Nixon's policies in Vietnam, but put nothing of themselves on the line to back up their support. This is not a disguised argument in favor of the war, but rather an indictment of those young men who used their favored positions to avoid their responsibility to prevent military fiascoes such as My Lai and to save Vietnamese and American lives.

The Vietnam veterans have been additionally abused because while they were slugging it out in Vietnam their countrymen had a change of heart about the war, conceding in the opinion polls that it had been a "mistake." Thus, on a daily basis, the servicemen in Vietnam were not only required to confront the ultimate sacrifice of their individual lives, but also the burden that those who had acquiesced in the decisions to send them to Vietnam for ambiguous purposes were now having second thoughts about the war itself. And now we are putting the Vietnam veterans on a back shelf of our public conscience because they are a painful reminder of a mistake we would like to forget. Captain Max Cleland, who lost both arms and his right leg at Khe Sanh, gave a poignant description of his brothers' plight in testimony before the Senate Subcommittee on Veterans' Affairs in 1970:

To the devastating psychological effect of getting maimed, paralyzed, or in some way unable to re-enter American life as you left it, is added the psychological weight that it may not have been worth it, that the war may have been a cruel hoax, an American tragedy, that left a small minority of young American males holding the bag. These doubts go beyond just the individual involved. They affect his family, his friends, and many times his community. These psychological repercussions do not hit you right away. . . . The inevitable psychological depression after injury coupled with doubts that it may not have been worth it come months later, like a series of secondary explosions, long after the excitement of the battlefield is far behind, the reinforcement of your comrades-in-arms a thing of the past, and the individual is left alone with his injury and self-doubts.

We should not forget these men, who are living testimony of why we must act with wisdom and dispatch to overcome the consequences of our failure in Vietnam. Are we willing to do what is necessary to make sure that the men who have been scarred in body or spirit, or both, by the rigors of the war are not left alone to cope with the consequences of our military failure? They are our sons, and they *all* require love and understanding. To give them any less is to succumb to failure.

APPENDIX

National Security Study Memorandum Number 1, February 1969

FOLLOWING is the text of the draft summary of questions and responses included in National Security Study Memorandum 1. It was prepared by various government agencies in answer to questions submitted by presidential adviser Henry Kissinger and his staff.

A guide to the abbreviations and terms used in the text, in their order of appearance:

DRV—Democratic Republic of Vietnam (North Vietnam)

NVA—North Vietnamese Army

GVN—Government of Vietnam (South Vietnam)

VC—Vietcong

RVNAF—Republic of Vietnam Armed Forces (South Vietnamese forces)

SVN—South Vietnam

MACV—Military Assistance Command Vietnam (U.S. headquarters)

RF and PF—Regional Forces and Popular Forces (South Vietnamese local defense militia)

NLF—National Liberation Front (the Vietcong political organization)

Hamlet rating C—Moderately secure

Hoa Hao—South Vietnamese religious sect

Cao Dai—Another religious sect
CINCPAC—Commander-in-Chief Pacific
JCS—Joint Chiefs of Staff
OSD—Office of the Secretary of Defense
USG—U.S. Government
NIE—National Intelligence Estimate
DIA—Defense Intelligence Agency
KIA—Killed in action
ARVN—Army of the Republic of Vietnam (South Vietnamese Army)
DMZ—Demilitarized zone
EA—East Asia (desk of State Department)
INR—Intelligence and Research (division of State Department)
HES—Hamlet Evaluation Survey (pacification program)

QUESTIONS

THE NEGOTIATING ENVIRONMENT

1. Why is the DRV in Paris? What is the evidence?
   Among the hypotheses:
   a. Out of weakness, to accept a face-saving formula for defeat.
   b. To negotiate the withdrawal of U.S. (and NVA) forces, and/or a compromise political settlement, giving a chance for NLF victory in the South.
   c. To give the U.S. a face-saving way to withdraw.
   d. To undermine the GVN and U.S./GVN relations, and to relieve U.S. military pressure on both North and South Vietnam.
   e. Out of desire to end the losses and costs of war on the best terms attainable.
2. What is the nature of the evidence, and how adequate is it, underlying competing views (as in the most recent NIE on

this subject, with its dissenting footnotes) of the impact of various outcomes in Vietnam within Southeast Asia?

3. How soundly based is the common belief that Hanoi is under active pressure with respect to the Paris negotiations from Moscow (for) and Peking (against)? Is it clear that either Moscow or Peking believe they have, or are willing to use, significant leverage on Hanoi's policies? What is the nature of evidence, other than public or private official statements?

4. How sound is our knowledge of the existence and significance of stable "Moscow" and "Peking" factions within the Hanoi leadership, as distinct, for example, from shifting factions, all of whom recognize the need to balance off both allies? How much do we know, in general, of intraparty disputes and personalities within Hanoi?

THE ENEMY

5. What is the evidence supporting various hypotheses, and the overall adequacy of the evidence, relating to the following questions:

   a. Why did NVA units leave South Vietnam last summer and fall?

   b. Did the predicted "third-wave offensive" by the NVA/VC actually take place? If so, why did it not achieve success?

   Among the hypotheses:

   1) Response to VC/NVA battle losses, forcing withdrawal or passivity.

   2) To put diplomatic pressure on the U.S. to move to substantive talks in Paris.

   3) To prepare for future operations.

   4) To prepare for pressure of U.S. and allied operations.

6. What rate of NVA/VC attrition would outrun their ability to replenish by infiltration and recruitment, as currently calculated? Do present operations achieve this? If not, what force levels and other conditions would be necessary? Is there any evidence they are concerned about continuing heavy losses?

7. To what relative extent do the U.S./RVNAF and the NVA/ VC share in the control and the rate of VC/NVA attrition; i.e., to what extent, in terms of our tactical experience, can heavy losses persistently be imposed on VC/NVA forces despite their possible intention to limit casualties by avoiding contact?

Among the hypotheses:

a. Contact is predominantly at VC tactical initiative, and we cannot reverse this; VC need suffer high casualties only so long as they are willing to accept them, in seeking contact.

b. Current VC/NVA loss rates can be maintained by present forces—as increases X% by Y additional forces—whatever the DRV/VC choose to do, short of further major withdrawal.

8. What controversies persist on the estimate of VC Order of Battle; in particular, on the various categories of guerrilla forces and infrastructure? On VC recruiting, and manpower pool? What is the evidence for different estimates, and what is the overall adequacy of the evidence?

9. What are NVA/VC capabilities for launching a large-scale offensive, with "dramatic" results (even if taking high casualties and without holding objectives long), in the next six months, e.g., an offensive against one or more cities, or against most newly "pacified" hamlets? How adequate is the evidence?

10. What are the main channels for military supplies for the NVA/VC forces in SVN, e.g., Cambodia and/or the Laotian panhandle? What portion of these supplies come in through Sihanoukville?

THE SOUTH VIETNAMESE ARMED FORCES

10A. What differences of opinion exist concerning the extent of RVNAF improvement and what is evidence underlying different views, e.g., compare recent CIA memo with MACV views. For example:

a. Which is the level of effective, mobile, offensive operations? What results are they achieving?

b. What is the actual level of "genuine" small-unit action in ARVN, RF, and PF; i.e., actions that would typically be classed as such within the U.S. Army and, in particular, offensive ambushes and patrols? How much has this changed?

c. How much has the officer selection and promotion system, and the quality of leadership, actually changed over the years, as distinct from changes in paper "programs"? How many junior officers hold commissions (in particular, battlefield commissions from NCO rank) despite lack of a high school diploma?

d. What known disciplinary action has resulted from ARVN looting of civilians in the past year, e.g., the widespread looting that took place last spring?

e. To what extent have past "anti-desertion" decrees and efforts lessened the rate of desertion? Why has the rate recently been increasing to new highs?

f. What success are the RF and PF having in providing local security and reducing VC control and influence in rural populations?

11. To what extent could RVNAF—as it is now—handle the VC (main force, local forces, guerrillas), with or without U.S. combat support to fill RVNAF deficiencies, if all NVA units were withdrawn:

a. If VC still had Northern fillers?

b. If all Northerners (but not regroupees) were withdrawn?

12. To what extent could RVNAF—as it is now—also handle a sizable level of NVA forces:

a. With U.S. air and artillery support?

b. With above and also U.S. ground forces in reserve?

c. Without U.S. direct support, but with increased RVNAF artillery and air capacity?

13. What, in various views, are the required changes—in RVNAF command, organization, equipment, training and incentives, in political environment, in logistical support, in U.S. modes

of influence—for making RVNAF adequate to the tasks cited in questions 9 and 10 above? How long would this take? What are the practical obstacles to these changes, and what new U.S. moves would be needed to overcome these?

PACIFICATION

14. How much, and where, has the security situation and the balance of influence between the VC and NLF actually changed in the countryside over time, contrasting the present to such benchmarks as end-61, end-63, end-65, end-67? What are the best indicators of such change, or lack of it? What factors have been mainly responsible for such change as has occurred? Why has there not been more?

15. What are the reasons for expecting more change in the countryside in the next two years than in past intervals? What are the reasons for not expecting more? What changes in RVNAF, GVN, U.S., and VC practices and adaptiveness would be needed to increase favorable change in security and control? How likely are such changes, individually and together? What are the obstacles?

16. What proportion of the rural population must be regarded as "subject to significant VC presence and influence"? How should hamlets rated as "C" in the Hamlet Evaluation System —the largest category—be regarded in this respect? In particular, what proportion in the provinces surrounding Saigon? How much has this changed?

17. What number of verified numbers of the Communist political apparatus (i.e., People's Revolutionary Party members, the hard-core "infrastructure") have been arrested or killed in the past year? How many of these were cadre or higher than village level? What proportion do these represent of total PRP membership, and how much—and how long—had the apparatus been disrupted?

18. What are the reasons for believing that current and future efforts at "rooting out" hard-core infrastructure will be—or will not be—more successful than past efforts? For example,

for believing that collaboration among the numerous Vietnamese intelligence agencies will be markedly more thorough than in the past? What are the side-effects (e.g., on Vietnamese opinion) of anti-infrastructure campaigns such as the current "accelerated effort," along with their lasting effect on hard-core apparatus?

19. How adequate is our information on the overall scale and incidence of damage to civilians by air and artillery, and looting and misbehavior by RVNAF?

20. To what extent do recent changes in command and administration affecting the countryside represent moves to improve competence, as distinct from replacement of one clique by another? What is the basis of judgment? What is the impact of the recent removal of minority-group province and district officials (Hoa Hao, Cao Dai, Montagnard) in their respective areas?

THE POLITICAL SCENE

21. How adequate is our information, and what is it based upon, concerning:

    a. Attitudes of Vietnamese elites not now closely aligned with the GVN (e.g., religious leaders, professors, youth leaders, professionals, union leaders, village notables) toward: participation—if offered—in the GVN; likewise (given "peace") for the NLF or various "neutralist" coalitions; toward U.S. intent, as they interpret it (e.g., U.S. plans for ending the war, perceived U.S. alignments with particular individuals and forces within Vietnam, U.S. concern for various Vietnamese interests).

    b. Patterns of existent political alignments within GVN/RVNAF and outside it—reflecting family ties, corruption, officers' class, secret organizations and parties, religious and regional background—as these bear upon behavior with respect to the war, the NLF, reform and broadening of the GVN, and responses to U.S. influence and intervention.

22. What is the evidence on the prospects—and what changes in conditions and U.S. policies would increase or decrease them —for changes in the GVN toward: (a) broadening of the government to include participation of all significant non-Communist regional and religious groupings (at province and district levels, as well as cabinet); (b) stronger emphasis, in selections and promotion of officers and officials, on competence and performance (as in the Communist Vietnamese system) as distinct from considerations of family, corruption, and social (e.g., educational) background, and support of the GVN, as evidenced (e.g., by reduced desertion) by willing alignment of religious, provincial, and other leaders with the GVN, by wide cooperation with anti-corruption and pro-efficiency drives?

23. How critical, in various views, is each of the changes in question 22 above to prospects of attaining—at current, reduced, or increased levels of U.S. military effort—either "victory" or a strong non-Communist political role after a compromise settlement of hostilities? What are the views of the risks attendant to making these changes, or attempting them; and, to the extent that U.S. influence is required, on U.S. practical ability to move prudently and effectively in this direction? What is the evidence?

U.S. MILITARY OPERATIONS

24. How do military development and tactics today differ from those of six to twelve months ago? What are the reasons for these changes, and what has this impact been?

25. In what different ways (including innovations in organization) might U.S. force-levels be reduced to various levels, while minimizing impact on combat capability?

26. What is the evidence on the scale of effect of B-52 attacks in producing VC/NVA casualties? In disrupting VC/NVA operations? How valid are estimates of overall effect?

27. What effect is the Laotian interdiction bombing having:
    a. In reducing the capacity of the enemy logistic system?

b. In destroying material in transit?
28. With regard to the bombing of North Vietnam:
   a. What evidence was there on the significance of the principal strains imposed on the DRV, e.g., in economic disruption, extra manpower demands, transportation blockages, population morale?
   b. What was the level of logistical through-put through the southern province of NVN just prior to the November bombing halt? To what extent did this level reflect the results of the U.S. bombing campaign?
   c. To what extent did Chinese and Soviet aid relieve pressure on Hanoi?
   d. What are current views on the proportion of war-essential imports that could come into NVN over the rail or road lines from China, even if all imports by sea were denied and a strong effort were made to interdict ground transport? What is the evidence?
   e. What action has the DRV taken to reduce the vulnerability and importance of Hanoi as a population and economic center, e.g., through population evacuation and economic dispersal?

SUMMARY OF RESPONSES

The Situation in Vietnam

The responses to the questions posed regarding Vietnam show agreement on some matters as well as very substantial differences of opinion within the U.S. government on many aspects of the Vietnam situation. While there are some divergencies on the facts, the sharpest differences arise in the interpretation of those facts, the relative weight to be given them, and the implications to be drawn. In addition, there remain certain areas where our information remains inadequate.

There is general agreement, assuming we follow our current strategy, on the following:

1. The GVN and allied position in Vietnam has been strengthened recently in many respects.

2. The GVN has improved its political position, but it is not certain that the GVN and other non-Communist groups will be able to survive a peaceful competition with the NLF for political power in South Vietnam.

3. The RVNAF alone cannot now, or in the foreseeable future, stand up to the current North Vietnamese-Vietcong forces.

4. The enemy have suffered some reverses but they have not changed their essential objectives and they have sufficient strength to pursue these objectives. We are not attriting his forces faster than he can recruit or infiltrate.

5. The enemy is not in Paris primarily out of weakness.

The disagreements within these parameters are reflected in two schools in the government with generally consistent membership. The first school, which we will call Group A, usually includes MACV, CINCPAC, JCS, and Embassy Saigon, and takes a hopeful view of current and future prospects in Vietnam within the parameters mentioned. The second school, Group B, usually includes OSD, CIA, and (to a lesser extent) State, and is decidedly more skeptical about the present and pessimistic about the future. There are, of course, disagreements within agencies across the board or on specific issues.

As illustration, these schools line up as follows on some of the broader questions.

• In explaining reduced enemy military presence and activities, Group A gives greater relative weight to allied military pressure than does Group B.

• The improvements in RVNAF are considered much more significant by Group A than Group B.

• Group A underlines advancements in the pacification program, while Group B is skeptical both of the evaluation system used to measure progress and of the solidity of recent advances.

• In looking at the political scene, Group A accents recent improvements while Group B highlights remaining obstacles and the relative strength of the NLF.

• Group A assigns much greater effectiveness to bombing in Vietnam and Laos than Group B.

Following is a summary of the major conclusions and disagreement about each of six broad areas with regard to Vietnam: the negotiating environment, enemy capabilities, RVNAF capabilities, pacification, South Vietnamese politics, and U.S. military operations. . . .

THE NEGOTIATING ENVIRONMENT

(Questions 1–4)

There is general U.S. government agreement that Hanoi is in Paris for a variety of motives, but not primarily out of weakness; that Hanoi is charting a course independent of Moscow, which favors negotiations, and of Peking, which opposes them; and that our knowledge of possible political factions among North Vietnamese leaders is extremely imprecise. There continues wide disagreement about the impact on Southeast Asia of various outcomes in Vietnam.

Why Is the DRV in Paris?

Various possible North Vietnamese motives for negotiating are discussed, and there is agreement that the DRV is in Paris for mixed reasons. No U.S. agency responding to the questions believes that the primary reason the DRV is in Paris is weakness. All consider it unlikely that Hanoi came to Paris either to accept a face-saving formula for defeat or to give the U.S. a face-saving way to withdraw. There is agreement that Hanoi has been subject to heavy military pressure and that a desire to end the losses and costs of war was an element in Hanoi's decision. The consensus is that Hanoi believes that it can persist long enough to obtain a relatively favorable negotiated compromise. The respondents agree that the DRV is in Paris to negotiate and to undermine GVN and USG relations and to provide a better chance for FV victory in the South. State believes that increased doubt about winning the war through international political pressure also played a major role. Hanoi's ultimate goal of a unified Vietnam under its control has not changed.

Vietnam Impact on Southeast Asia

There continues to be a sharp debate between and within agencies about the effect of the outcome in Vietnam on other nations. The most recent NIE on this subject (NIE 50-68) tended to downgrade the so-called "domino theory." It states that a settlement which would permit the Communists to take control of the government in South Vietnam, not immediately but within a year or two, would be likely to bring Cambodia and Laos into Hanoi's orbit at a fairly early state, but that these developments would not necessarily unhinge the rest of Asia.

The NIE dissenters believe that an unfavorable settlement would stimulate the Communists to become more active elsewhere and that it will be difficult to resist making some accommodation to the pressure then generated. They believe, in contrast to the Estimate, these adjustments would be relatively small and insensitive to subsequent U.S. policy.

Factors entering into the judgments are estimates of (1) Hanoi's and Peking's behavior after the settlement; (2) U.S. posture in the regions; (3) Asian leaders' estimates of future U.S. policy; (4) the reactions of the area's non-Communist leaders to the outcome in Vietnam; (5) vulnerabilities of the various governments to insurgency or subversion; and (6) the strengths of opposition groups within each state.

The assessments rest more on judgments and assumptions than on tangible and convincing evidence, and there are major disagreements within the same department. Within the Defense Department, OSD and DIA support the conclusions of the NIE, while Army, Navy, and Air Force Intelligence dissent. Within State, the Bureau of Intelligence supports the NIE while the East Asian Bureau dissents.

Both the majority and the dissenters reject the view that an unfavorable settlement in Vietnam will inevitably be followed by Communist takeovers outside Indo-China.

Indeed, even the dissenter, by phrasing the adverse results

in terms such as "pragmatic adjustments" by the Thais and "some means of accommodation" leave it unclear how injurious the adverse effects would be to U.S. security.

Moscow and Peking Influence

There is general government agreement on this question. Peking opposes negotiations while Moscow prefers an early negotiated settlement on terms as favorable as possible to Hanoi. Neither Peking nor Moscow have exerted heavy pressure on Hanoi and for various reasons they are unlikely to do so, although their military and economic assistance give them important leverage. (CIA notes that "in competing for influence Peking and Moscow tend to cancel out each other.") For its own reasons Hanoi's tendency in the last year has been in the Soviet direction. However, the Hanoi leadership is charting its own independent course.

Hanoi Leadership Factions

There is agreement that knowledge of the existence and significance of possible factions within the Hanoi leadership is imprecise. There are differences of opinion within the leadership on tactics as opposed to ultimate objectives but there are not stable "Moscow" and "Peking" factions. The Hanoi leadership will form different alignments on different issues. The attempts by the agencies to ascertain the position of various North Vietnamese leaders on specific issues show the imprecision of our information and analysis. For example, different agencies set forth sharply conflicting identifications of the position of individual leaders such as Giap on particular questions.

THE ENEMY

(Questions 5–10)

Analyses of various enemy tactics and capabilities reveal both significant agreements and sharp controversies within the Government. Among the major points of consensus:

• A combination of military pressures and political tactics explains recent enemy withdrawals and lower levels of activity.

• Under current rules of engagement, the enemy's manpower pool and infiltration capabilities can outlast allied attrition efforts indefinitely.

• The enemy basically controls both sides' casualty rates.

• The enemy can still launch major offensives, although not at Tet levels, or, probably, with equally dramatic effect.

Major controversies include:

• CIA and State assign much higher figures to the VC Order of Battle than MACV, and they include additional categories of VC/NLF organization.

• MACV/JCS and Saigon consider Cambodia (and specifically Sihanoukville) an "important enemy supply of guerrilla and local forces activity," and State agrees there has been a "relative decline." Both agree that among the reasons are the heavy casualty rates, manpower problems and loss of cadres. But according to Embassy evaluators, the main factor is that "the VC are husbanding their resources to give themselves the option of a 'climaxing' offensive." State notes that to support the VC counterpacification campaign and their "Liberation Committees," "the Communists may feel that a demonstrably strong blow against the pacification program would have wide repercussions particularly at a time of optimistic Allied claims about pacification successes."

NVN/VC Manpower

It is generally agreed that the NVN/VC manpower pool is sufficiently large to meet the enemy's replenishment needs over an extended period of time within the framework of current rules of engagement. According to the JCS, "The North Vietnamese and Vietcong have access to sufficient manpower to meet their replenishment needs—even at the high 1968 loss rate of some 291,100—for at least the next several years. . . . Present operations are not outrunning the enemy's ability to replenish by recruitment or infiltration." Enemy losses of 291,000 in 1968 were roughly balanced by infiltration and recruitment of 298,000.

North Vietnamese manpower assets include 1.8 million physically fit males aged 15 to 34, of whom 45 percent are in the regular forces (475,000) and paramilitary (400,000) forces. 120,000 physically fit males reach draft age each year and 200,000 military and labor personnel have been freed by the bombing halt from defensive work. The potential manpower pool in SVN is estimated to be half a million men and recruitment, while down, is running at approximately 3,500 per month. Enemy maintenance of the current commitment of 300,000 new men per year requires that the Allies inflict losses of 25,000 KIA per month, or 7,000 more than the current rate. MACV considers current Allied force levels adequate to inflict such casualties if the enemy chooses to engage.

The enemy's employment of economy of forces tactics since the fall of 1968 and intelligence evidence reflect the enemy's concern about his 1968 level of losses, which if continued another year would mean nearly 100 per cent yearly attrition of his full-time fighters and nearly total North-Vietnamization of local fighting forces in South Vietnam. He is judged unlikely to undertake the heavy losses of a major offensive unless he believes he could thereby achieve a breakthrough in Allied will power in Vietnam or Paris. Yet, without a VC/NVA offensive on the scale of Tet 1968, the JCS believe "it will be exceedingly difficult in 1969 for allied forces to attrite the enemy at 1968 levels."

Control of NVA/VC Attrition

There is general agreement with the JCS statement: "The enemy, by the type action he adopts, has the predominant share in determining enemy attrition rates." Three-fourths of the battles are at the enemy's choice of time, place, type, and duration. CIA notes that less than 1 percent of nearly two million allied small unit operations conducted in the last two years resulted in contact with the enemy and, when ARVN is surveyed, the percentage drops to one-tenth of 1 percent. With his safe havens in Laos and Cambodia, and with carefully chosen tactics, the enemy has been able during the last four years to double his combat forces, double the level of infiltration, and increase the scale and intensity of the main-force war even while bearing heavy casualties.

VC Order of Battle

Considerable disagreement is evidenced concerning the estimates of Vietcong order of battle, the categories of guerrilla forces, recruiting manpower pool, and quality of the data. MACV includes only enemy personnel engaged in offensive military actions and estimates enemy strength at 327,000. Moreover, CIA and State consider categories of paramilitary and administrative service to be indispensable to the enemy's military effort and population control, and extrapolate a total range of 435,000 to 595,000 men. State, noting that the MACV estimate results from adding up so-called "hard" field intelligence figures for main-force, local, and guerrilla forces, believes CIA's extrapolation is developed more realistically from the totality of evidence. OSD presents both MACV and CIA estimates, pointing out that the differences in overall strength presented by the two are not sufficient to cause a change in overall strategy (though, as CIA notes, they could have a bearing on peace terms).

Recruiting figures vary for reasons similar to the divergencies on strength. Monthly VC recruitment is estimated at 8,500 in 1966, 7,500 in 1967, double the 1967 rate during the first quarter of 1968 and dropping sharply after the Tet offensive to approximately 3,500 per month. CIA estimates a smaller drop than MACV. Saigon reports that the last six months reflect a reduced level of recruitment, citing as evidence GVN expansion, reduction in VC standards, VC attempts to improve existing cadre, increased use of NVA fillers in VC units, and GVN mobilization effectiveness.

NVA/VC Capabilities for a Large-Scale Offensive

All agree that (as recent events have borne out) the enemy has a capability for a large-scale offensive against cities, bases, and/or villages in the accelerated pacification program if he wishes to bear the heavy casualties that would result. Allied countermeasures and pre-emptive capabilities make it highly unlikely that such an attack would have an impact on the scale of the Tet offensive of 1968. Further, the enemy would have to weigh the effect of such an offensive on the Paris talks and on the risk of touching off a resumption of bombing in North Vietnam.

NVA/VC Supply Channels

There is general agreement that the main channels for military supplies reaching enemy forces in the northern areas of South Vietnam (I, II, and a part of III Corps) are the Laos Panhandle and the DMZ. Considerable disagreement exists as to the channel of supplies for the southern part of South Vietnam (part of III and all of IV Corps). MACV, CINCPAC, JCS, and Embassy point to Cambodia. MACV believes that no large shipments of ordnance are coming into IV Corps via Laos and that Cambodia has during the last two years become a major source of supplies for this region, with 10,000 tons of arms going through Sihanoukville to the border between October 1967 and September 1968. CIA disagrees strongly, especially with regard to the importance of Sihanoukville. It estimates that the external resupply requirement of IV Corps is three tons of combat-related material a day and that this comes across two Cambodian border points and the South China sea coast of South Vietnam. CIA notes numerous factors which it believes cast doubt on the importance of the Sihanoukville channel.

OSD summarizes without comment the national level CIA/DIA estimates for total enemy external daily supply requirements of 80 tons; 34 tons come from Laos, 14 tons across the DMZ, and 32 tons from Cambodia (of which 29 tons involve mainly food and other noncombatant goods).

THE SOUTH VIETNAMESE ARMED FORCES

(Questions 10A–13)

The emphatic differences between U.S. agencies on the RVNAF outweigh the points of agreement. There is consensus that the RVNAF is getting larger, better equipped, and somewhat more effective. And all agree that it could not now, or in the foreseeable future, handle both the VC and sizable NVA forces without U.S. combat support. On other major points there is vivid controversy. The military community gives much greater weight to RVNAF statistical improvements while OSD and CIA highlight remaining obstacles, with OSD being the most pessimistic. Paradoxically, MACV/CINCPAC/JCS see RVNAF as being less capable against the VC alone than does CIA.

RVNAF Capabilities Against the Enemy

The Vietnamese Armed Forces (RVNAF) are being increased in size and re-equipped to improve their ground combat capability. The best measure of this improvement is the RVNAF's expected performance against a given enemy threat. However, there is a paradoxical divergence in agency views on the RVNAF ability to handle the internal VC without U.S. assistance. State (both EA and INR) and CIA—who generally rate RVNAF improvement and effectiveness lowest among the respondents, and who accept the highest estimates of overall VC strength— believe that "without any U.S. support . . . ARVN would at least be able to hold its own and make some progress against the VC unsupported by the NVA" (i.e., the VC without NVA fillers, though with regroupees).

In contrast is the view of MACV/CINCPAC/JCS, who rate RVNAF effectiveness highest, who accept the lowest estimates of VC armed strength, and who (unlike CIA and State) do not consider VC irregular forces to be part of the VC military thrust. But the military community believes that without U.S. combat support, in opposing VC main and local forces without any NVA units or fillers, RVNAF "would have to reduce the number of offensive operations and adopt more if a defensive posture," resulting in "loss of control by the government of Vietnam over substantial rural areas." Thus, MACV/CINCPAC/JCS believe that RVNAF would not be able to cope with purely indigenous VC forces without U.S. combat support until the completion of the modernization in 1972.

OSD, however, believes that a number of major reforms are required, in addition to the current modernization program, if this goal is to be met. "It is unlikely that the RVNAF, as presently organized and led, will ever constitute an effective political or military counter to the Vietcong."

All agencies agree that RVNAF could not, either now or even when fully modernized, handle both the VC and a sizable level of NVA forces without U.S. combat support in the form of air, helicopters, artillery, logistics, and some ground forces.

RVNAF Improvements

There is consensus that RVNAF forces are now much larger (826,000) than in December 1967 (743,000), and will be further increased to 876,000, with the greatest increases in manpower given to the popular and regional forces needed for local security. The RVNAF is also better equipped. All regular combat units have M-16 rifles and are beginning to achieve increases in their own artillery and helicopter support. Militia (393,000 of the total RVNAF strength in December 1968) have 100,000 M-16 rifles and are scheduled to receive 150,000 more in 1969. MACV has stepped up its training efforts by forming 353 mobile teams in 1968 to train and advise the militia.

Moreover, all agencies agree that overall RVNAF capabilities, number of operations, and effectiveness increased during 1968. Data presents a mixed picture in some areas, but it is clear that the larger number of enemy killed by RVNAF resulted from better effectiveness (more kills per 1,000 troops), along with higher kill ratios, as well as increased force size. In spite of these statistical improvements (which CIA in particular finds unreliable indicators), RVNAF is best thought of as a force which enlarged its contribution in 1968 within a total allied effort which also expanded. The modernization program, just beginning to have a high impact on the field, promises that results will continue to increase so long as RVNAF receives backbone in the form of a U.S. ground combat presence.

RVNAF Problems

RVNAF faces severe motivation, leadership, and desertion problems. The officer problem is mixed in politics and little has been done to correct it. Poor leadership and motivation contributes to regular ground combat forces deserting (net) at an annual rate of 34 percent of their strength (gross rate one-third of the divisions is more than 50 percent). Total RVNAF desertions (net) are equivalent to losing one ARVN division per month.

Thus, OSD does not believe that current expansion and re-equipment programs are sufficient to make RVNAF into an effective fighting force because major political and military actions are required that are not now emphasized. OSD considers essential action to recognize and reward combat leadership and development of a favorable attitude of the military towards their own people which will result in acceptance and support of the government by its citizens.

JCS, CINCPAC, MACV, and State feel that, without such changes, RVNAF is making reasonable progress toward development as a self-sufficient force able to hold its own against an internal VC threat. OSD and CIA feel that RVNAF is making limited progress and many of RVNAF's weaknesses are uncorrected.

OSD suggests the possibility of cutting costs and U.S. losses by reducing U.S. forces as RVNAF reaches milestones in the modernization program. This plan is contingent on the enemy force stabilizing at a reduced level of threat. A plan to withdraw one U.S. division during mid-1969 has been discussed with President Thieu, who responded favorably. Allied troop reductions are dependent on progress in RVNAF improvement, changes in enemy forces, and a manageable battlefield and pacification situation in South Vietnam.

PACIFICATION

(Questions 14–20)

Two well-defined and divergent views emerged from the agencies on the pacification situation in South Vietnam. One view is held by MACV and Embassy Saigon and endorsed by CINCPAC and JCS. The other view is that of OSD, CIA, and State. The two views are profoundly different in terms of factual interpretation and policy implications. Both views agree on the nature of the problem, that is, the obstacles to improvement and complete success. What distinguishes one view from the other is each's assessment of the magnitude of the problem, and the likelihood that obstacles will be overcome.

The Two Views

The first group, consisting of MACV/JCS/Saigon, maintains that "at the present time, the security situation is better than any time during period in question," i.e., 1961 to 1968. MACV cites a "dramatic change in the security situation," and finds that the GVN controls three-fourths of the population. JCS suggests that the GVN will control 90 percent of the population in 1969. The second group, OSD/CIA/State, on the other hand, is more cautious and pessimistic; their view is not inconsistent with another Tet offensive-like shock in the countryside, for example, wiping out the much-touted gains of the 1968 accelerated pacification program, or with more gradual erosion. Representing the latter view, OSD arrives at the following conclusions:

1. "The portions of the SVN rural population aligned with the GVN are apparently the same today as in 1962 (a discouraging year); 5,000,000 GVN aligned and nearly 3,000,000 VC aligned.

2. "At the present, it appears that at least 50 percent of the total rural population is subject to significant VC presence and influence."

CIA agrees, and State (INR) goes even further: "Our best estimate is that the VC have a significant effect on at least two-thirds of the rural population."

The Major Issues

After removing population control changes attributable to urban migration (which has brought more people under GVN control than pacification), the two views differ by the magnitude of up to about one-sixth of the South Vietnamese people, i.e., 2 to 3 million. The second group places these people in a contested category, yet to be secured by the GVN, while the first group maintains that these 2 to 3 million people are already under GVN control.

The substance of the argument is evident on the next page. Using HES data for 1967–68, the chart [not reproduced] shows that the optimistic interpretation leaves only 26.7 percent of SVN's population to be pacified as of November 1968. The conservatives think 41.3 percent of the population has yet to be pacified. More importantly, the second view shows little pacification progress over the period except for the gains of the accelerated pacification campaign (APC) program, and they dispute these gains. State, OSD, and CIA maintain that the October–December APC acquisition of 9.4 percent of the population is an exaggerated claim because these gains were achieved by cutting minimal force levels to one-third of previously accepted levels. These agencies, therefore, argue that the APC gains have stood only because the NLF has not challenged them, and they believe it is "quite likely" the gains will be contested in the coming months.

If the APC gains are removed, the substance of the long-term debate emerges clearly. The chart then shows that according to the second view, pacification programs have registered no progress over 1967–68 and before. The first view records only slight progress over the 1966–68 period. It is further seen that the second view places the chart's pacification line much lower. For example, in August 1968 the first group says 65.8 percent of the population was under GVN control; the second group places only 49.9 percent in the GVN category. The source of this difference is a dispute over the value of the HES composite indicator, which is really an average of eighteen indicators, few of which have anything to do with security. (There is a strong case for abolishing an overall composite indicator from HES and either utilizing the subindicators on a category basis, e.g., security, political, and economic development, or using the category data within a newly devised system. Despite all its shortcomings, HES has provided useful data and the small amount of analysis available is very helpful, although large areas of analytical ground remain to be covered.)

The second group arrives at their estimate by allocating the contested population on the basis of security criteria alone. According to their view, in the fall of 1968 at least one-half of South Vietnam's population was subject to a significant NLF presence; for the first group, this figure was one-third.

By neither view can pacification be said to have progressed much in the last three years (at least, prior to the last few months). Nor does either view promise anything close to complete success within several years. If the 1967–68 pacification rate (including the debated APC gains) is sustained, the first interpretation implies that it will take 8.3 years to pacify the 4.15 million contested and VC population of December 1968; the second view implies pacification success in 13.4 years.

It is noteworthy that the gap in views that does exist is largely one between the policy makers, the analysis, and the intelligence community on the one hand, and the civilian and military operators on the other.

The policy implications of the disagreement could hardly be more divergent. One view sees a high probability of GVN success and generally applauds the GVN's performance. It finds that the GVN has been ineffective at times, but that it has not been negligent, and overall progress has been most satisfactory. The policy implications of this view are more of the same, gradual U.S. pressure and wholehearted U.S. support.

The other view leads to a radically different policy. The GVN has failed in the countryside. The rural population situation has not changed significantly and certainly not at a rate which will free us of noticeable burdens within two to five years. We may even be overextended in the rural areas and open to a damaging VC counterattack. The implied policy recommendations would call for voicing considerable displeasure at the GVN's rural performance; establishing realistic rural goals for the GVN; penalizing the GVN if these goals are not achieved; and devoting a greater effort to promoting a GVN/VC rural political acommodation on, for example, a district or village basis.

Lesser Issues

In 1968, 16,776 members of the Vietcong infrastructure (VCI) were neutralized, 87.1 percent of whom were low-level functionaries. Anti-VCI operations showed major improvements but did not seriously harm the VCI.

All agencies agreed that the Phoenix program was long overdue and potentially very valuable. The respondents agreed that it is too early for a thorough assessment of the Phoenix program, and they predict it is unlikely to cause the NLF major problems in 1969. Embassy Saigon noted that Phoenix bears close watching with respect to the attitudes of rural population, attitudes toward the American sponsors, and a potentially deleterious effect on the possibilities for a rural accommodation.

Every agency except MACV/JCS agrees that the available data on war damage to the civilian population is inadequate. Using limited data which showed that 7 percent of the reporting hamlets were affected by friendly-caused war damages, CIA concluded "the rural hamlets take a tremendous beating." The responses received suggest that this is a very serious problem in need of further U.S. government attention and analysis.

Recent GVN personnel changes were found by all agencies to have brought a significant upgrading in the average quality of GVN officials. Nonetheless, corruption, favoritism, and neglect of the populace's problems were still seen as major GVN shortcomings. There was no conclusive evidence that the 1968 personnel changes harmed the GVN's relations with minority groups.

THE POLITICAL SCENE

(Questions 21–23)

This section on the political situation can be boiled down to three fundamental questions: (1) How strong is the GVN today? (2) What is being done to strengthen it for the coming political struggle with the NLF? (3) What are the prospects for continued non-Communist government in South Vietnam?

The essence of the replies from U.S. agencies is as follows:

(1) Stronger recently than for many years but still very weak in certain areas and among various elites. (2) Some steps are being taken but these are inadequate. (3) Impossible to predict but chancy at best.

Within these broad thrusts of the responses there are decided differences of emphasis among the agencies. Thus MACV/ JCS and Saigon, while acknowledging the problems, accent more the increasing stability of the Thieu regime and the overall political system, the significance of the moves being made by the GVN to bolster its strength, and the possibility of continued non-Communist rule in South Vietnam given sufficient U.S. support. CIA and OSD, on the other hand, while acknowledging certain progress, are decidedly more skeptical and pessimistic. They note recent political improvements and GVN measures but they tend to deflate their relative impact and highlight the remaining obstacles. State's position, while not so consistent or clear-cut, generally steers closer to the bearishness of OSD and CIA.

The Present Situation

We have a great quantity of information on Vietnamese politics but the quality is suspect. It varies greatly by elite and level and is usually sounder for broad groups than factions or individuals. In addition, we are dealing with a nascent constitutional system and public opinion is often manipulated.

Non-Communist elements rally in times of common danger from the Communist threat, but otherwise generally engage in a perpetual struggle for power. Most elites may be willing to participate in the GVN but their motives are often more self-serving than nationalistic. In their view toward the military struggle, Northerners are most insistent on military victory, central Vietnamese the most war-weary, Southerners the most ambiguous. Firm support for GVN comes from most military elements, Catholics, and the bureaucratic and merchant classes. The major problem for the GVN remains in the rural villages where the VC are strongest. Opposition also comes from uncertain Buddhist, youth, union, and army elements. Various ethnic and religious minorities, while often anti-Communist, are not strongly tied to the GVN.

In reading the Vietnamese political scene, one must keep in mind that pragmatism, expediency, war weariness, a desire to remain unaligned and end up on the winning side are all common features. So are family loyalty, corruption, social immobility, and clandestine activities.

OSD points out (and a recent Saigon cable corroborates this view) that there has been a noticeable shift recently by many non-Communists toward acceptance of the NLF in some capacity as part of an eventual political settlement. Most elites would want to minimize the Communist influence in the government.

South Vietnamese attitudes toward the U.S. are varied and ambivalent. Our presence is seen as a necessary evil to forestall a Communist takeover. Our involvement is viewed with a mixture of gratitude, shame, and suspicion. In any event, recent events, especially the Paris talks, have made it clear to the Vietnamese that the U.S. commitment is not open-minded and that some withdrawals will probably come soon.

GVN Political Actions

All agencies agree that there has been substantial progress in broadening the government; all except OSD see significant movement against corruption; and all agree that political mobilization is both the [material missing] advancement based on merit, and there are many other political steps needed. In general, all these factors will be increasingly important as the U.S. reduces its military effort. Such a reduction might stimulate political progress but it will also entail risks. As noted earlier, there is some ambiguity as well as differences of view about the proper U.S. role in SVN politics. State and Saigon caution against undue U.S. involvement and pressure, while MACV/JCS place greater emphasis on the use of our leverage in effecting needed reforms.

No agency clearly forecasts a "victory" over the Communists, and all acknowledge the manifold problems facing the GVN as we withdraw. However, MACV/JCS stress the need for continued U.S. support. OSD and State believe that only a compromise settlement is possible and emphasize GVN self-reliance. CIA states that progress in SVN has been sufficiently slow and fragile that substantial U.S. disengagement in the next few years could jeopardize all recent gains.

JCS and OSD each list their essential conditions for cessation of hostilities. While they agree on certain elements, the JCS look toward continued U.S. support to assure the sovereignty of the GVN while OSD requires only that the South Vietnamese be free to choose their political future without external influence.

U.S. MILITARY OPERATIONS

(Questions 24–28)

The only major points of agreement with the U.S. government on these subjects are:
- The description of recent U.S. deployments and tactics.
- The difficulties of assessing the results of B-52 strikes, but their known effectiveness against known troop concentrations and in close-support operations.
- The fact that the Soviets and Chinese supply almost all war material to Hanoi and have enabled the North Vietnamese to carry on despite all our operations.

Otherwise there are fundamental disagreements running throughout this section, including the following:
- OSD believes, and MACV/JCS deny, that there is a certain amount of "fat" in our current force levels that could be cut back without significant reduction in combat capability.
- MACV/JCS and, somewhat more cautiously, CIA ascribe much higher casualty estimates to our B-52 strikes.
- MACV/JCS assign very much greater effectiveness to our past and current Laos and North Vietnam bombing campaigns than do OSD and CIA.
- MACV/JCS believe that a vigorous bombing campaign could choke off enough supplies to Hanoi to make her stop fighting, while OSD and CIA see the struggle even against unlimited bombing.

U.S. Deployments and Tactics

In early 1968, MACV moved the equivalent of two divisions from II and III Corps to northern I Corps. This deployment was a defensive reaction to the threat of a major NVA siege of Khe Sanh and the coastal lowlands. With the further enemy offensives in February and May, U.S. forces throughout the country (except for I Corps) were pulled back into screening positions around SVN's major cities and used to push the VC forces out. Since then, the two U.S. divisions redeployed to I Corps have been returned to III and IV Corps, and the heavily populated upper Delta.

Until late 1968, allied (particularly U.S.) efforts were directed largely against enemy main forces through large (1,000 men or more) unit operations. With the recent withdrawal of NVA main force units from SVN, U.S. units have been able to operate in smaller units and with more emphasis on the enemy's infrastructure and support apparatus. Though no U.S. units are currently in direct support of pacification, the deployment of U.S. units in SVN's populated areas and the change in tactics has, MACV asserts, helped improve pacification progress.

U.S. Force Reductions

MACV/JCS and OSD agree that there is no way of reducing U.S. force levels in Vietnam without some reduction in combat capability. However, OSD argues that withdrawing some U.S. logistics headquarters, construction, or tactical air personnel may not have any significant effect on U.S. combat effectiveness. For instance, OSD concludes that because of the halt in bombing North Vietnam, the U.S. needs neither as many interdiction aircraft as we now have nor our full force of three Navy carriers off North Vietnam. OSD also believes certain tactical innovations might make some troop cutbacks possible. MACV/JCS feel that while some of the above elements would help to minimize loss of combat capability, in general, significant reductions in our force levels will proportionately reduce our combat capability.

OSD also thinks that U.S. forces could be reduced as the

RVNAF improves and expands. By their estimates, the ongoing RVNAF improvement plan might free up to about 15 U.S. battalions and their support units by mid-1969, without a decrease in total allied force capability. This projection assumes that RVNAF combat effectiveness increases along with their combat capability. In their responses, MACV/JCS do not consider this question.

B-52 Effectiveness

All agencies acknowledge that sound analysis of the effectiveness of B-52 strikes is currently impossible for several reasons. The consensus is that some strikes are very effective, some clearly wasted, and a majority with indeterminate outcome.

There is agreement that B-52 strikes are very effective when directed against known enemy troop concentrations or in close support of tactical operations, and have served to disrupt VC/NVA operations.

There are sharp differences on casualty estimates. While the JCS estimate that about 41,000 enemy were killed in 1968 by the B-52 strikes, OSD believes that perhaps as few as 9,000 were. The difference is that OSD, unlike MACV/JCS, find that B-52 strikes against suspected enemy infiltration routes or base camps (50 percent of 1968's sorties) are much less effective than close-support strikes. CIA cites a variety of casualty estimates and considers it impossible to select one, but believes it is apparent that B-52 strikes have become a significant factor in the attrition of enemy forces.

The Laos and North Vietnam Interdiction Campaign

The MACV/JCS and State/CIA/OSD fundamentally disagree over whether our bombing campaign either prior to or after November has reduced the enemy's through-put of supplies so that the enemy in South Vietnam receives less than he needs there. The MACV/OSD think it has suceeded; State/CIA/OSD think it has failed.

Post-November Campaign

Since early November, MACV has attempted to reduce the logistic capacity of the enemy by blocking the two key roads near the passes from NVN into Laos. MACV finds it has effectively blocked these roads 80 percent of the time and therefore caused less traffic to get through. OSC/CIA/State agree that enemy traffic on the roads attacked has been disrupted. However, they point out that the enemy uses less than 15 percent of the available road capacity, is constantly expanding that capacity through new roads and bypasses, and our air strikes do not block but only delay traffic.

Besides blocking the roads, our bombing destroys material in transit on them. JCS/MACV and OSD/CIA agree that we destroy 12 percent to 14 percent of the trucks observed moving through Laos and 20 percent to 35 percent of the total flow of supplies in Laos. To MACV/JCS, the material destroyed cannot be replaced so that our air effort denies it to the VC/NVA forces in South Vietnam. In complete disagreement, OSD and CIA find that the enemy needs in SVN (ten to fifteen trucks of supplies per day) are so small and his supply of war material so large that the enemy can replace his losses easily, increase his traffic flows slightly, and get through as much supplies to SVN as he wants to in spite of the bombing.

Pre-November Campaign

Prior to November 1968, we bombed in southern North Vietnam as well as Laos. The MACV/JCS find that this campaign reduced the flow of supplies into Laos greatly and that this flow increased greatly after the bombing halt. The OSD/CIA agree that traffic followed this pattern, but argue that it was caused by normal seasonal weather changes, not our bombing policy. Comparing 1967 traffic to 1968 traffic, they find that prior to the bombing halt, 1968's supply throughout was higher than 1967's and that, after the halt, it followed its normal seasonal patterns.

Alternative Campaign

All agencies agree that Chinese and Soviet aid has provided almost all the war material used by Hanoi. However, OSD/CIA and MACV/JCS disagree over whether the flow of aid could be reduced enough to make a difference in South Vietnam. If all imports by sea were denied and land routes through Laos and Cambodia attacked vigorously, the MACV/JCS find that NVN could not obtain enough war supplies to continue; in total disagreement, OSD and CIA believe that the overland routes from China alone could provide NVN enough material to carry on, even with an unlimited bombing campaign.

Index

Ackley, Gardner, 141–42
Actium, Battle of, 31
Agriculture, Department of, 162
Aiken, George D., 20
Air Force, U.S., 76
Alba, Duke of, 38–39
Albert, Archduke, 40
Amherst, Lord, 47
Anson County (N.C.), 163
An t-Oglach, 63
Antonine Emperors, Era of, 35–36
Armed Forces Drug Abuse Control Act (1971), 78–79
Armed Forces Management, 94
Armenia, 33–34
Army, British, see British Army
Army, U.S., 76, 85, 104, 162
  domestic political surveillance and, 108–9
  Corps of Engineers, 162
  Special Forces unit, 163–64
  see also Military, U.S.
Army of the Republic of Vietnam (ARVN), 24–25
  see also National Security Study Memorandum No. 1
Augustus, 31–33
Auxiliaries, 67–68

Bankston, Edward E., 93
Barnett, Correlli, 41
Beaslai, Piaras, 70
Beddingfield, Robert, 98
Belgium, 41
Bell, Alan, 64–65
Bennett, L. Arnold, 95
Bill of Rights, 110
Black and Tans, 67–68
Bolovens plateau, 24
Britain, ancient, 35
British Army, Irish Rebellion and, 54–55, 57–59, 60, 66, 67, 69, 70
British Intelligence Service, 65
Brown, H. Rap, 92
Bruce, David K., 23, 24
Brussels, 38
Bundy, McGeorge, 151
Bureaucracy, federal, 110–17, 141

Cade, Jack, 44
Califano, Joseph, 111
Caligula, 33
Calley, William, 84
Cambodia, 22, 23, 25, 26, 172
Camp Lejeune (N.C.), 92–93

Canada, 68
Carmichael, Stokely, 92
Carroll, George, 9–10
Chapman, Leonard F., Jr., 93–94
Charles V (of the Holy Roman
Empire), 36–37
Charleston (S.C.), 50
China, *see* People's Republic of
China
Chou En-lai, 24
Churchill, Winston, 69
Citizen armies, 30
Civilian Conservation Corps
(CCC), 162
Clarke, Tom, 59–61
Clausewitz, Karl von, 28–29
Cleaver, Eldridge, 92
Cleland, Max, 173–74
Cold War, 83
Collins, Michael, 55–56, 59, 60–
61, 63–68, 71–72
Columbia Broadcasting System
(CBS), 110
Combined Action Platoon (CAP),
96
Commoner, Barry, 148
Common Market, *see* European
Common Market
"Conflicting outcomes" theory,
145–48
Congress, U.S., 107, 115, 118,
119, 120, 139, 142, 143,
155, 170–71
military drug abuse question
and, 78–80
Cornwallis, Charles, 50
Corporations, 140–41, 142, 144
Court of Blood, 38
Craig, Sir James, 68
Cronkite, Walter, 155
Curtis, Edward E., 46

Custer, George C., 32
Czechoslovakia, 34

Dacia, 33, 34–35
Dail Eireann, 54, 61–62, 63, 65–
66, 68
Defense, Department of, 75, 78,
95, 113, 115, 161, 164,
165
Democratic convention (1972),
128
Densen-Gerber, Judianne, 80–81
Draft system, 88, 127, 173
Drug abuse, military establish-
ment and, 75–82

Easter Rising (1916), 56–59, 60,
72
Economic Stabilization Program,
139–40ff.
Economy, the, failure in Vietnam
and
inflation, recession and governmental controls, 139–44
"conflicting outcomes" theory,
144–46
poverty and, 146–47
pollution and, 147–48
Egypt, 31
82nd Airborne Division, 86
Eire, 53n
Eisenhower, Dwight D., 19
England, 38
Hundred Years' War and, 43–
45
see also Great Britain
Ervin, Sam J., Jr., 108
"Ethic of responsibility," 125
European Common Market, 154–
55

Failure, 15–16
  see also Military failure
Federal Bureau of Investigation (FBI), 109, 110
Federal Pay Comparability Act (1970), 110*n*
Federal Reserve System, 143
Ferdinand (of Spain), 42
Finch, Robert, 115
Fisher, Herbert, 30–31
Formigny, 44
Fort Bragg (N.C.), 86, 163
Fragging, 87–89, 99
France, 38, 43–44, 47, 49
  Nazi occupation of (1940), 58
Free, Lloyd A., 142
Free State, 53*n*
Fulbright, J. William, 20, 21

George III (of England), 46–47, 48, 49
Germaine, Lord, 49*n*
Germans, ancient, 31–32
Gibbon, Edward, 35–36
Glenn Springs (S.C.), 163
Gough, Major General, 70–71
Government, *see* U.S. Government
Government of Ireland Act (1920), 69
Great Britain, 43
  American Revolution and, 45–51
  see also England; Ireland
Great Depression, 15
Great Silent Majority, 132–36
Green Beret murder case, 74
Gruenther, General, 101
Guerrilla warfare, 29*n*, 38–40, 43, 49, 70
  see also Irish Republican Army

Hadrian, 35–36
Hadrian Wall, 35
Health, Education, and Welfare, Department of (HEW), 115
Henry V (of England), 43–44
Henry VI (of England), 44–45
Hessians, 46, 48–49
Hitler, Adolf, 34
Hoke County (N.C.), 163
Holland, 41
  see also Netherlands
Hollier, Louis S., 92–93
Home Rulers, 69*n*
Hoover, J. Edgar, 109
House Armed Services Committee, Subcommittee on Drugs, 76, 77
Housing and Urban Development, Department of (HUD), 115
Howe, Lord, 47
Huguenots, 38
Hundred Years' War, 43–45

Iberian peninsula, 31
India, 158
Indians, American, 49
Indochina Peace Conference, 23
Industrial Revolution, 50
Insurrectional warfare, 53, 67
Interest groups, 117–18
Interior, Department of the, 162
Ireland, 43, 51
  Britain's military failure in (1916–22), 51–73
  Sinn Fein/IRA political and military strategy, 53–55
  rebel leadership, 55–61 *passim*
  Easter Rising, 56–57

(*Ireland continued*)
  execution of rebel leaders,
    57–59, 60
  Sinn Fein election tactics,
    61–62
  Sinn Fein's declaration of
    war, 63
  IRA guerrilla tactics, 63–67
  British reaction to, 67–68
  peace negotiations and settle-
    ment, 68–72
Irish Civil War (1922–23), 56
Irish Parliamentary Party, 61
Irish Rebellion, *see* Ireland
Irish Republican Army (IRA), 53–
  55, 56, 59, 63–67, 70, 71,
  72
Irish Republican Brotherhood
  (IRB), 53–54, 63
Isabel Clara Eugenia, 40
Isabella (of Spain), 42
Isolationism, 155, 157–59

Jack Cade's rebellion, 44
Japan, 160
Jarres, plain of, 24
Jellinek, Frank, 58
Johnson, Haynes, 84
Johnson, Lyndon B., 19, 26, 47,
  83, 109, 111, 119, 127,
  131, 139
Joint Chiefs of Staff, 25n
  see also National Security Study
    Memorandum No. 1
Jordan, 86
Justice Department, Internal Se-
  curity Division of the, 108,
  109

Kennedy, John F., 19, 109, 112
Khaki Election, 61
Kilmainhan jail, 60
King, Martin Luther, 91–92, 131

Kissinger, Henry, 21, 22, 25, 26,
  29n
  see also National Security Study
    Memorandum No. 1
Korean War, 91, 101, 133
Koza (Okinawa), 97

Labor, Department of, 115
Lame Deer (Montana), 163–64
Laos, 22, 23, 24–25, 26
League of Nations, 15
Lerma, Duke of, 41
"Let's Unite on Vietnamization,"
  21–22
Life of Michael Collins, The, 70
"Limited war" strategy, 28, 29
Linden, Eugene, 87
Littauer, Raphael, 26n
Little Big Horn, Battle of, 32
Lloyd George, David, 68, 70
Local government, 164, 165–69
Longbinh, 81–82
Long Cheng, 24

MacArthur, Douglas, 28
Macquis, 58n–59n
Macready, General, 69, 70
McAuliffe, General, 101
McCarthy, Joseph, 18
McGonigal, Richard A., 96–97,
  98
McNamara, Robert S., 91, 112–
  14, 139, 151
Maine, 44
Malcolm X, 92
Management and Budget, Office
  of, 171
Mansfield, Mike, 20, 21
Margaret of Parma, 38
Marine Corps, U.S., 75–76, 85,
  93–94, 96
  see also Military, U.S.

Marius, 30
Martyrology, 57*ff*.
Mataxis, Theodore, 161
Maxwell, Sir John, 57
Mercenaries, 46, 48–49
Military, British
  Hundred Years' War and, 44–45
  American Revolution and, voluntary recruitment question, 47–48
Military, U.S., 20, 72, 133
  reaction to Vietnamization program, 21–22
  failure in Vietnam and, 74–75, 103–5
    drug abuse question, 75–82
    dissent question, 82–89
    junior officer leadership vacuum, 84–86
    fragging, 87–89
    race relations problems, 89–98
    command and the "passive-aggressive" response, 98–100
    officer selection/promotion process, 100–103
  all-volunteer force, cost of, 111
  Vietnam veterans' attitude toward, 137
  use of in a domestic/civil action role, 161–69
  see also Military failure
Military defeat, 29
Military failure, 15, 16–18, 148–49
  defined, 28–30
  case studies of
    Roman Empire, 30–36
    Spain's war in the Netherlands, 36–43

England and the Hundred Years' War, 43–45
England and the American Revolution, 45–51
  see also Ireland, British military failure in
"last best chance to avoid" principle, 62
prevailing objective conditions, avoidance of failure and, 72–73
"conflicting outcomes" theory and, 144–48
overcoming consequences of Vietnam failure, 150–54
projected outcomes and possible courses of action, 154–60
repairing institutions: use of military in domestic/civic action role, 161–69
treatment of Vietnam veterans, 169–74
  see also Economy, the; Military, U.S.; Public, American; U.S. Government; Vietnamization
Military-industrial complex, 74, 141
Miller, Arthur R., 108
Monagan, John S., 77–79
Montana, 164
Moorer, Thomas H., 25*n*
Moors, 42
Moriscos, War Against the, 42
My Lai massacre, 74, 151, 173

National Assembly of Ireland, 54
National Association for the Advancement of Colored People (NAACP), 90
National Liberation Front, 23

National Security Study Memorandum No. 1 (NSSM 1), 21, 26, 175–205

negotiating environment: questions, 176–77; answers, 185–87

the enemy: questions, 177–78; answers, 187–91

South Vietnamese Armed Forces: questions, 178–80; answers, 191–94

pacification: questions, 180–81; answers, 194–98

political scene: questions, 181–82; answers, 198–201

U.S. Military Operations: questions, 182–83; answers, 201–5

Naval Reserve Construction Battalion (Seabees), 164–65

Navy, U.S., 85

Nazis, occupation of France by (1940), 58

Nero, 33

Netherlands, war against Spain, 36–43

New York, 50

New York American, 64

New York Times, The, 21

Nixon, Richard M., 28, 127, 154, 159, 173

decision to end war, 19–21, 26–27

purpose behind Vietnamization, 22

China policy, 24, 25

"carpet bombing" decision, 27

war on heroin, 78–79

political surveillance question, 108–10

federal bureaucracy and, 110n, 113, 115

economic policies, 139–40ff.

disabled Vietnam veterans and, 170–71

see also Vietnamization

Normandy, 44

North, Lord, 46–47

North Carolina, 163

Northern Ireland, 52n–53n, 68, 69n

North Vietnam, 19, 23–24, 25, 26, 27, 29n, 155, 158, 170, 172

see also National Security Study Memorandum No. 1

Nuclear weapons, 154, 158

Organized labor, 140, 141

Ostend, siege and capture of, 40

Pakistan, 158

Palmer, General, 102

Pannonia, province of, 31

Paris Commune (1871), 57, 58

Paris Commune of 1871, The, 58

Paris peace talks, 23, 24

see also National Security Study Memorandum No. 1

Parliament, English, 61–62, 67, 69n

Parthia, 34–35

Pathet Lao, 24

Penobscot (Maine), 50

Pentagon, procurement of war materials by, 112

Pentagon Papers, 17, 18

People's Republic of China, 24, 25, 125, 154, 155

Philip II (of Spain), 36, 37–40

Philip III (of Spain), 40–42

Philippines, 29

Phillips, Alison, 66

Pitt, William, 51

Polaris system, 112
Pollution, 146, 148
Poverty, 146–47
President's Committee on Equal
  Opportunity in the Armed
  Forces, 90
Press gangs, 48
Prisoners of War (POWs), 23, 150,
  169–70, 171
Professional armies, 30–31
Project Nation Building, 163
Public, American, failure in Viet-
  nam and, 123–24, 138
youth and the political process,
  124–30
turnout in 1972 elections,
  128–29
adults and the political process,
  130–36
anti-war activists, 130–32
Great Silent Majority, 132–
  36
Vietnam veterans and the mili-
  tary system, 136–37
Pueblo affair, 74
PX scandals, 100

Race relations, military establish-
  ment and, 89–98
Raspberry, William, 171
Reed, Walter, 162
Rehnquist, William H., 108
Reich, Charles, 130
Republic of Ireland, 53n, 68–69
Reserve Army Field Hospital Unit,
  165
Reserve Officer Training Corps,
  84
Revolution, American, 43, 45–51,
  91, 136
Revolution in Ireland, The, 66
Rhode Island, 50

Rickover, Hyman, 112
Roman Empire, 30–36
Rostow, Walt, 151
Royal Irish Constabulary, 66, 67
Rumania, 33
Rusk, Dean, 88

Salary Reform Act (1962), 111
Security, national, 107–10
"Selling of the Pentagon," 101
Senate Foreign Relations Com-
  mittee, 20
Shatan, Chaim F., 171
Shaw, George Bernard, 55
Silent Majority, *see* Great Silent
  Majority
Sinn Fein, 53, 54, 55, 59, 61–63,
  65, 67, 68, 70, 72
"Six Counties," 52n
Slavery, 15
Son Tay prison camp, 23
Southern Ireland, 53n, 69
South Vietnam, 19, 20–21, 22,
  23–24, 25, 26, 81–82, 125,
  140, 155, 158, 172
see also National Security Study
  Memorandum No. 1
Soviet Union, 154, 155, 157, 160
Spain, 31, 36–43
Spanish-American War, 29
Spinola, Ambrogio, 41
State of the Nation, 142
State of the World message (Nix-
  on, 1971), 24
Suffolk, Earl of, 44
Sullivan, William, 109
Swords and Plowshares, 101

Taylor, Maxwell D., 21–22, 101–2
Tercios, 38, 41
Tet Offensive (1968), 57
Thailand, 26

Thai troops, 24
Thiers, Adolphe, 58
Third World, 153
Tiberius, 31–32
Tolson, John J., 163
Tongue River Indian Reservation, 164
Total Package Procurement (TPP), 112–13
Trajan, 33–35, 43
Third Republic, 58
Truman, Harry S., 19, 90
Truscott, Lucian K., III, 100–1, 104
Twelve Years' Truce (1609), 41, 42
Twenty-six Counties, 53n

Ulster, 52n
Ulster Unionists, 69n
"U.S. Air War in Vietnam," 26n
U.S. Government, failure in Vietnam and
    domestic reform question, 106–7
    internal security and political surveillance question, 107–10
    federal bureaucratic problems, 110–17, 118, 119–20
    economic problems, 117
    interest group proliferation, federal programs and, 117–18
    electorate's attitude toward political process, 118–19
    dissent and civil liberties, 119–21
    crisis of confidence, 121–22
    see also Economy, the; Public, American

Urban League, 90

Varus, Publius Quintilius, 32
Veterans Administration, 171
Viet Cong, 26, 29n
    see also National Security Study Memorandum No. 1
Vietnam/Vietnam War, 15, 16–18, 19–27, 47, 49, 50n, 67n
    de-escalation of, drug abuse in the military and, 76–77
    see also Military failure; National Security Study Memorandum No. 1; Vietnamization
Vietnamization, 28
    military's reaction to, 21–22
    purpose behind, 22
    diplomatic-offers-and-threats strategy, 22, 23–24
    "to ignore" strategy, 22, 25
    military-lunges-and-lulls strategy, 22–23, 24–25
    Laos incursion failure, effect of on, 25
    de-escalation question, air war and, 25–26
    bombing statistics, 26
    Nixon's decision the right one, 26–27

Wage and price controls, 139–40, 141, 142–44
Wage comparability, federal bureaucracy and, 110–12
War of the Roses, 45
Washington, George, 46, 50
Watts, William, 142
Webb, Beatrice, 55

Webb, Sydney, 55
Weber, Max, 125
Wedemeyer, General, 102
Welfare reform, 147
Western Europe, 160
Westmoreland, William C., 47, 50n, 151
World War I, 29, 44, 69, 101

World War II, 29, 59n, 102, 133, 144

Yorktown, British surrender at, 50–51

Zinberg, Norman E., 77